THE PRINT REVOLUTION

GROUNDBREAKING TEXTILE DESIGN IN THE DIGITAL AGE

THE PRINT REVOLUTION

GROUNDBREAKING TEXTILE DESIGN IN THE DIGITAL AGE

Foreword by
Mary Katrantzou

Tamasin Doe

GOODMAN

Published in 2013 by Goodman
An imprint of the Carlton
Publishing Group
20 Mortimer Street
London W1T 3JW

10 9 8 7 6 5 4 3 2 1

Text © Tamasin Doe 2013
Foreword © Mary Katrantzou 2013
Design © Carlton Books 2013

A CIP catalogue record for this book is
available from the British Library.

ISBN 978 1 84796 069 6

Printed in China

PREVIOUS PAGE Sketch,
Midnight Diner design, Clover Canyon,
Spring/Summer 2013: Collage technique
featuring "warped" neon image framed by
classic foulard design.

RIGHT Embellished jacket and
trousers, Topshop Unique, Spring/
Summer 2011: Inspired by the sun
shining through flowers on a summer's
day and mythical creatures, including
Pegasus and fairies, the collection's prints
were both ethereal and surreal.

Contents

Foreword   6

Introduction   10

The Designers   16

Agi & Sam   18

Michael Angel   24

Antoni & Alison   34

Basso & Brooke   42

Hussein Chalayan   52

Tsumori Chisato   58

Clover Canyon   64

Giles Deacon   70

Dolce & Gabbana   76

Fabitoria   82

Holly Fulton   90

Givenchy   98

Josh Goot   102

Prabal Gurung   108

Christopher Kane   114

Jen Kao   120

Mary Katrantzou   126

Helmut Lang   136

Alexander McQueen   144

Erdem Moralioglu   150

Peter Pilotto   158

Prada   164

Proenza Schouler   166

Masha Reva   170

Romance Was Born   178

Jonathan Saunders   188

Topshop Unique   194

Iris van Herpen   200

Dries Van Noten   204

Matthew Williamson   210

Designer Directory   216

Index   217

Acknowledgements   222

Foreword by Mary Katrantzou

Print allows a woman to filter beauty through her wardrobe. All my prints are constructed through digital technology and I use precision engineering to flatter the female form. I am interested in the way that printed textiles can morph the shape of a woman's body. My work is about perception as well as it is about print, the two work alongside each other to allow women to wear the beauty found in design, in a subversive way. When designing, I think of scale because of the limitations I have to address that are imposed by the physical form of a dress. It provides a canvas for me to create, but print as a means of applied design is so transferable beyond these constraints and I often like to turn an idea on it's head and subvert a reality to a hyper reality. In the past, print was often small in scale or an abstraction of geometric colour, to satisfy the needs of pattern and motif creation. A paisley, a floral, a motif from inanimate objects was created to beautify a dress and decorate it with colour and pattern. But what happens when you take that scale and enlarge it to define a second skin for a woman, that is as definitive as a cut or a drape? A typewriter is relevant to the body when it's placed to become the wearer's collarbone and its properties are thus changed through this process of appropriation. In my first collection I took the notion of a woman wearing perfume and turned it on its head, where the perfume was placed on the dress as a life-size print to extenuate a woman's hourglass silhouette. It was a new way of looking at print which I feel allowed print to set itself beyond being just a trend.

Print nowadays can liberate a woman to dress in a way that they couldn't dress before, indulging in fashion to define their taste and aesthetic and communicating more about their design affinities. In recent decades, the world has experienced a second boom in private contemporary art collections and that has also been the case in what people choose to wear. They choose to wear something unique that defines their taste in design and with print you can communicate that directly; consumers and designers alike are able to create their own distinctive worlds through the medium of print. In my work I look at still-life photography and filtered beauty in design to create an assemblage of images sometimes found, sometimes created from scratch and collage them together to create a fictitious world that is novel. This collage then acts as a guide to inspire painting through pixels to create a print, and once a print is created, you can transfer it to any means of design and explore its properties. It excites me to build a world where a print can travel through a designer's curated eye. I'm fascinated by the fine balance of creating something that is your own and what our role has become as curators, bringing elements together and refining their properties to give birth to a new existence.

Designers are trying to use digital technology not just to physically create their designs but to portray them in different, modern and groundbreaking ways. My prints may be decorative but I see myself as a minimalist at heart because of the simplicity of shape and its relation to print. Studying architecture made me very aware of the digital construction and technicality of engineering in design, which has informed my design direction with prints. In my design and thought process I am constantly building from the foundations of my initial inspiration and I often use architectural methods of accumulating designs at phase one. Engineering my prints is very mathematical and technical and it allows me to envision a 3-D shape around the body, sculpting a second skin for a woman. A print is designed around the garment, and the garment simultaneously around the print; they have to work together in direct synergy, there is no room for error! Digital print allows me to experiment with print in a way that fine art and other methods could not. I use my mouse as my paintbrush and it opens up a huge spectrum for possibility; I can create possibility out of impossibility, surrealism out of realism and vice versa. I want the work to live on and be appreciated by others and used as a vehicle to open a discussion in the hands of others, explored and expressed through different scales and media. Print and the printed image are strong advocates of communication and we can now do that on a global scale. The work communicates in a very direct way because of its visual strength and can open up different avenues for discussion and further creation. That accessibility that didn't exist in the past, I believe, refines and trains the eye and ultimately leads to an evolution and a heightened importance of applied design to form perception.

OPPOSITE Fashion designer Mary Katrantzou (centre) with models wearing her digital designs.

OVERLEAF Mary Katrantzou, Autumn/Winter 2013–14, ready-to-wear.

Introduction

Fashion is about change and the quest for newness. The speed and restless energy of digital culture has made it an ideal vehicle for creating and transmitting new fashion ideas. The most curious and innovative designers spearheaded the move toward digital technologies when they started to emerge generally in the late 1980s. It was some time, however, before the technology developed that could turn this revolutionary new field of science and data into a seductive product. Print turned out to be the first breakthrough area for designers.

Silk-screen printing, either by hand or machine, has been the standard method of printing in the modern fashion age. It is a process that requires each colour to have its own screen or roller, a stencil through which dye is applied to fabric. Each extra colour or screen raises the cost to the designer. Consequently the richest multi-hued fabrics made this way have traditionally been available only to the most expensive fashion houses and their customers.

Digital printing works in the same way as a desktop ink-jet printer. It delivers a limitless palette of colours directly across the width of the fabric, or on to high-quality transfer paper that is then applied to a base material using a heat press. Whereas screen-printing requires a repeat pattern, a single design that is repeatedly printed for the length of the fabric, the digital process doesn't. It can print a single image along the length of the material, limited only by the size of the digital file with which it is created.

The machines used to print fabrics emerged from those designed to print banners and paper. They have multiplied tenfold the amount of fabric that can be printed during a single day. Alison Smart, print director at RA Smart, a UK-based print company that works across every print discipline, says, "The flexibility afforded by the digital process is breathing new freedoms into the creative process. We're able to produce a single metre of 40 designs in a 40-metre print-run for example, which can then be easily split, as opposed to a 40-metre run of the same design. This, coupled with the fact that bright colours can be used at a fraction of the cost compared to screen methods, is encouraging innovative use of colour and intricate design at all levels."

Some established designers were quick to embrace and explore digital printing while others avoided it over concerns that the finished quality wouldn't be suitable for the designer market. There certainly have been issues in terms of quality; in the past textiles printed with traditional methods have compared favourably to digital ones. The fidelity of a print, for example, has taken a long time to match up with what a designer can produce on their computer screen. Getting a decent black has been another major challenge for ink-jet printing. Designers have experimented with slowing the printing machines to ensure better coverage and for now there are limitations to what they can achieve. Also, digital printing is a flat process and textural effects such as flocking and foiling are not yet possible.

The relationship between a designer and his or her print has both deepened and, in some ways, become more remote. A print is researched, created and rendered as a digital file. It is then sent to a printer that, with minimal set-up and physical processes, can return the completed fabric in a fraction of the time it would previously have taken. This is a crucial advance for designers – the process of testing materials can make the difference between a successful collection and one that's less so – but it also removes a designer's physical relationship with the cloth. The more quickly a print can be produced, the greater control a designer will have over the finished piece, yet the artistry of physically applying ink to fabric is forfeited.

RIGHT Backstage, Topshop Unique, Spring/Summer 2011: An organic print is embellished with graduated gems to give texture and depth.

OVERLEAF, LEFT Column dress, Basso & Brooke, Spring/Summer 2010: Themed around Neo-pop and the work of artist Jeff Koons, the designers' prints emerged as "dream-like fantastical landscapes". Sinuous fabrics such as jersey and silk were used in tandem with the print and lines of the garment to create a "waterfall" of pattern.

OVERLEAF, RIGHT Detail, Mary Katrantzou, Spring/Summer 2012: Eline Le Callennec created this embroidery for the designer as an "... embellishment that complements the print using embroidery and beading as a shape and colour enlightener to the digital print".

This is just one way the digital revolution and its subsequent technologies have transformed the way fashion designers work. From advances made in microprocessors and file sharing to mobile communication, each development has presented designers with a new opportunity. Together they form a whole new dimension from within which to create. In particular Adobe's Photoshop and Illustrator programs have placed in their hands the tools they needed to bring textile design, traditionally a separate discipline, into their own studios.

The role of textile designer still exists, of course, although this now encompasses digital skills alongside established techniques such as screen-printing. For fashion designers, the reason for bringing print closer to the garment design is about exploring the interface between the two. This very often requires collaboration, especially around the need for graphic skills. Agape Mdumulla and Sam Cotton (Agi & Sam), Peter Pilotto and his partner Christopher de Vos, Bruno Basso and Christopher Brooke: all are partnerships that encompass fashion construction and print. Most however are less visible and exist within the studio. For example, Lee Alexander McQueen mentored his nephew artist Gary James McQueen, who went on to create some of the label's remarkable digital prints. Alexander McQueen is also the place where Jonathan Saunders first made his mark with a bird-of-paradise print for the designer's S/S 2003 *Irere* collection.

Most of the designers featured on the following pages now employ graphic artists, just as they have always worked with textile designers. The nature of a photographic image or painting shared through the medium of fabric actively invites this and together these partnerships have fashioned a brand new aesthetic. It blends traditional techniques such as collage with digitally-honed graphics. Often photography is processed to create dense patterns of saturated colour, an intense and dramatic effect.

One of the most significant techniques created by designers and their teams as a response to the new technologies has been engineered prints. These are created by printing an entire garment onto a single length of fabric ready for cutting and sewing. They appear as flat pattern pieces with the print already applied to the fabric. It is this method that creates the kaleidoscope or mirror effect so associated with digital textile printing. It is also one of the techniques through which designers are able to separate their work from more easily reproducible techniques.

Philip Delamore, director of the Fashion Digital Studio based at the London College of Fashion, started looking at engineered prints around 2001, inputting the paper patterns on his flatbed scanner and then combining the prints and patterns in Illustrator and Photoshop. As a practising textile designer he has experienced the entire digital print revolution. "Early on, I was working on digital prints as a consultant for designers. I would often have to 'un-digitize' them – try to achieve a screen-printed look with the technique – because digital print was regarded as inferior and that wasn't what designers were looking for. The full-blown digital aesthetic took a long time to develop.

"Like most technologies, there is a 'trickle-down' process. A new invention is used first by the military and then it may find an application within sports and eventually it emerges with a more general purpose for designers. The companies that develop them are usually targeting them at areas other than fashion so it takes a curious designer like Hussein Chalayan or Iris van Herpen to venture into a different field to find and use them."

With the surfaces intensely patterned, designers have more often chosen to simplify the lines of the garments themselves. Crisp, contemporary shapes

are used to equalize the effect of extreme print combinations. That isn't to say that those choices have been unimaginative. One of Mary Katrantzou's greatest commercial successes has been her bulbous lampshade skirts, designed for A/W 2011 (see pages 132–3). This architectural approach has proved to be a natural bedfellow for digital printing. Prints have often been engineered to mirror and enhance the dramatic lines beneath them.

Modernity may be the overwhelming response to digital printing but it can also be used to recreate archival textiles. The Colonial Williamsburg Foundation, in Virginia, used digital printing to recreate printed silk shantung from the eighteenth century. A swatch was simply repaired in Photoshop and printed for use on a period dress. It's a technique that has been used by designers looking to reimagine historical prints without the laborious and expensive process of having them re-drawn.

Many devotees of traditional printing methods maintain that digital printing lacks the spirit and individuality of the more human processes. It can also miss the sincerity of a print that has taken many stages to create. By way of response, designers have been enriching their digital prints with embellished details and overprinting. This injection of handcrafted work also gives digital printing the third dimension and texture it lacks. Eline Le Callennec specializes in textile embellishment and has worked for both Alexander McQueen and Katrantzou. "It's obvious that we are surrounded by digital technology. Everyone is able to use a laser-cutting machine or to print textiles online. That makes everyone a potential designer who can make products with industrial finishes. Designers have to be more than competitive – they have to be highly creative and bring new and fresh ideas to the market." Le Callennec uses a variety of hand-applied elements to "humanize" her own digital work, an amalgamation that takes us to yet another creative arena.

At the top of the market, designers are finding new ways to distinguish their work and further explore digital territory. Elsewhere digital printing is finding its way into the wider market as it becomes cheaper and printers are better able to provide the volume the high street requires. Topshop has a special place in the development of digital printing for mass-market use. Unique, its premium collection shown twice annually at London Fashion Week, sits precisely between the designer market that has been able to use digital print as a financially viable alternative to other print options and the high street, for which it has previously been too expensive (see also pages 194–9). Emma Farrow, head of design at Topshop, says, "Unique is a showcase for Topshop design in its purest form and in general its ideas and advances filter down into the main collections. We have been using digital printing as part of our main ranges for a few years now. At first it was quite difficult to get any in at an all-store level due to the higher costs, but over the years we have worked closely with our suppliers to get them set up with the right equipment to facilitate more cost-effective production at a digital level."

Digital printing machines are constantly being refined and developed – it is not unusual for a printing company to replace and upgrade their printers annually. The technologies, therefore, are constantly offering designers new opportunities. At the same time the resurgence in fashion print has also benefited traditional screen-printing in some respects. With the emphasis falling so heavily on print, designers have the scope to use and explore both areas of print. Hand printing of every kind is being re-assessed as the valuable and special process that it is.

Fleet Bigwood, a practising textiles designer, has taught the textiles pathway of the MA Fashion course at Central Saint Martins College of Arts and Design for over 20 years. During that time, many of fashion's brightest

luminaries have passed through its doors, including Katrantzou and McQueen. He believes that for all the excitement surrounding digital printing, designers need to understand a print's relationship with the material it decorates. "Digital printing has huge potential but it needs to be treated with sensitivity," he says. "There needs to be a harmony between the cloth and the print and that doesn't just happen. A designer needs to understand the fabric rather than treating it simply as a surface.

"The most successful designers in the field are the ones who don't simply scan in an image and print it – that's too easy. There needs to be more of a process than simply using Photoshop's mirror tool, otherwise the work will lack originality or purpose since plenty of people have done that before. We have to make things new."

Liberty has been at the forefront of commercial and art textile printing since the late nineteenth century. During that time it has collaborated with many designers, from Bill Blass to Vivienne Westwood. Emma Mawston, head designer at Liberty Art Fabrics, believes there is a place for a variety of techniques, so long as they are treated with equally high standards in terms of print mark and colour matching, as well as design. "I think digital printing and screen printing work wonderfully together in a collection enabling different effects and designs to be created. There are colours and tints that are not able to be created digitally only with screen printing and obviously vice versa."

One of the factors that may determine where printing develops more generally is its environmental footprint. The digital printing process uses half the ink of screen-printing methods and results in less waste being discharged. There is also no washing of screens or changing colours, so water consumption is reduced by almost half. The commercial imperative certainly points to the reduced wastage and cost of digital printing. Sam Cotton and his partner Agape Mdumulla regard the green aspect as indivisible from their design work. In particular they have focused on finding background fabrics that equal the potential of the new printers. "Digital print fabric bases have been quite limited," he explains. "This led us to source fabrics that could take the ink while at the time being a completely new composition... Having the opportunity to sublimation [transfer] print more cleanly than digital onto a wool emulation fabric that is made from 100 per cent recycled Coca-Cola bottles is really quite amazing."

The detonation of print within fashion has exposed the widest possible range of styles. For their label Antoni & Alison, Antoni Burakowski and Alison Roberts have been creating their highly individual prints for over 25 years. "We look at things in a new way, never trend led," says Burakowski. The team started to work with digital processes in 2002. "To most, a print is a print, but digital printing definitely has, if the artwork is 'considered', a 'wow factor' that can truly amaze. Digital print has grown up alongside computers and mobile phones, which are everywhere and used everyday and are forever evolving. Historically, to us, in fashion terms, it feels as relevant and like the new 'New Look' of 1947... which people either loved or hated but it did change fashion and cause an interest much more widely in fashion."

Print has undoubtedly experienced a revolution, and continues to do so. Armed with advanced materials, a limitless colour palette and new computer programs fashion designers are using the faster, cleaner world of digital printing to create a new visual language. As the digital printing industry improves old systems and develops new ones, designers are primed to exploit whatever it has to offer. So far their creative responses have been spectacular. Can they even exceed their astonishing output?

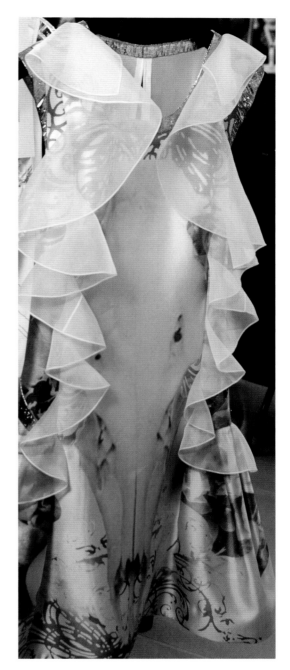

ABOVE Silk print dress, Prabal Gurung, Autumn/Winter 2012–13: In this design for a collection titled *Uncursed*, named after an exhibition by artist Yoko Ono, Gurung partners printed satin with organza ruffles. The collection evokes heaven and hell, this dress representing the former with its sheer silk frills framing the body like a halo.

OPPOSITE *Smoke* print, Topshop Unique, Spring/Summer 2011: Feathers, smoke and light flares are manipulated and layered to create a mysterious world inhabited by wraithlike creatures.

The Designers

Designers have generated the widest possible variety of creative responses to the digital processes now offered to them. Erdem and Dries Van Noten explore historical references and recreate them as new visions. Antoni & Alison investigates the limits of scale and ersatz texture. Others, including Mary Katrantzou and Basso & Brooke, have reinvented the concept of what a textile print can or should be through their uninhibited use of imagery.

Every season the technology develops and designers find new ways to embrace it. Whether their particular skill is a mastery of the endless colour palette offered by digital printing or the application of engineered prints to achieve a new zenith of creative effects, each of the designers featured here has distinguished themselves in the new print age.

LEFT Sketches, Clover Canyon, Autumn/Winter 2013–14: A multitude of prints forms a patchwork background to the collection's silhouettes. The theme, *Russia*, emerges through abstracted symbols of the country's Czarist and Soviet history, including crystal chandeliers, metro stations, Fabergé eggs and frozen Siberian lakes.

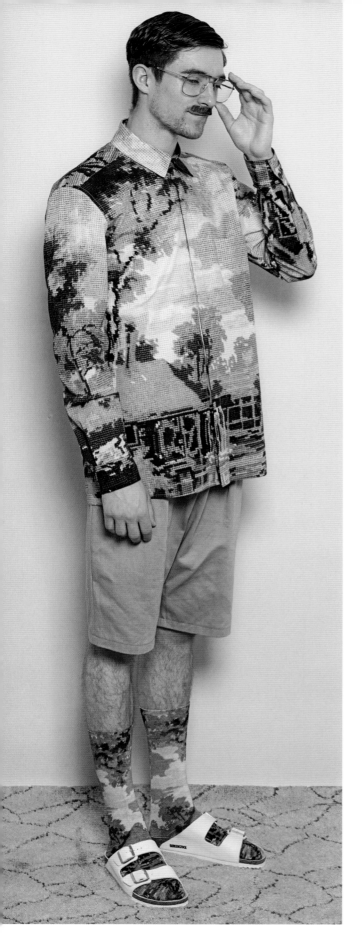

Agi & Sam

Agi & Sam is a partnership that brings together print and tailoring to create a very British vision. Humour and the traditions of Savile Row infuse the work of Agape Mdumulla and Sam Cotton, both trained at art school – Mdumulla in fashion design and Cotton in illustration.

After graduation, Cotton learned the theory of production, colour and fabric while he was producing print for Alexander McQueen, Karl Lagerfeld and Armand Basi. Mdumulla, meanwhile, trained with a London tailor before spending a year with Alexander McQueen working alongside the menswear team. It was at McQueen that the pair met and started their own label in 2010.

They may be trained in separate areas but at the start of each collection, both work across the process. "We design the prints and garments together, it's an important part of the way the company works and how our aesthetic is amalgamated," explains Cotton. "We start by drawing up silhouettes and playing around with garment ideas. After a rough base has been drawn, we can then start dropping print ideas onto the silhouettes and playing around with our colour board." It is only at this stage that the pair part to concentrate on their specialisms. "After the designs have been drawn up we both work within our personal disciplines. I will actuate the prints and Agi actuates the pattern cutting," explains Cotton.

Print is central to each collection rather than simply being a nuance or contrast to solid colour or texture. "I think because print is so visual and can be at times very literal it is definitely a great way to really express your design ideas," says Cotton. "I think because our ideas are so playful, it's a great way to express something quite fun without having to make a conscious effort to actually change the garments. Print allows the clothes to stay very wearable structurally and at the same time adds personality to our fabrics."

The menswear catwalk seasons have grown in prominence to the point where emerging brands for men are every bit as fêted as those for women. Agi & Sam certainly have their counterparts in womenswear, but the strength and individuality of their vision is equal to any.

"With a strong emphasis on entirely bespoke print and humour, we believe that fashion should never be taken too seriously." Agi & Sam

LEFT Printed shirt and socks, Agi & Sam, Spring/Summer 2013: Photographic prints of needlepoint bring a touch of louche comedy to Agi & Sam garments. Mdumulla and Cotton use colour and humour as a positive act designed to entertain and cheer.

OPPOSITE Suit and coat, Agi & Sam, Autumn/Winter 2012–13: A *pointilliste* effect is achieved with digital print to subvert the traditional tailored suit. The collection, humorously titled *Darwin's Theory of Why the Chicken Crossed the Road*, used fabrics made of recycled plastic bottles woven to replicate natural fabrics such as cotton and jersey.

ABOVE *Fox* print, Agi & Sam, Autumn/Winter 2013–14: *Fox* was
created for a collection inspired by the eccentric aristocrat Alexander Thynn, 7th
Marquess of Bath. The designers then played with the social aspects of British
country life; a fox gambols and does some hunting of his own.

ABOVE Needlepoint print, Agi & Sam, Spring/Summer 2013: A tongue-in-cheek print based on a bucolic millpond scene. Inspired by memories of their grandparents' living rooms, the designers digitized a vintage, crafted work, giving it new purpose.

Michael Angel

Since the debut of his collection in 2007, Australian-born Michael Angel has become known for creating refined, urban clothes – a magnet for sophisticated celebrities who prefer to reflect, rather than direct, trends. He says that his ideal client is "a creative woman who is not afraid to have her own idea of style", and Angel's collections combine confident edge with an easy-to-wear practicality. His contemporary, elegant shapes are decorated with equally slick digital prints, a focus for Angel who is also an artist that works with both digital and manual artwork.

Born and raised in Melbourne, Angel worked for the Australian brand SABA for eight years, organizing runway shows and marketing campaigns. In 2004 he moved to New York, where he initially worked as a stylist before morphing into a designer. His mirrored, head-to-toe prints quickly made their mark, but Angel has at times used the technique sparingly, preferring instead to use the prints as highlights in collections that focus on structure rather than surface.

Angel's instinct is for modernism. "How can I do what I do with prints and be a minimalist?" is the question he has asked himself. The answer is to keep his shapes pared or simple, even when they're also voluminous to showcase his prints. Swathes of luxuriously printed satin are used as a foil to solid jackets; blocky shifts are ideal backdrops for complicated surface designs. Often long in length, Angel's restrained aesthetic owes something to both the American sportswear and the Japanese design traditions.

Other designers work with photographic images and motifs but Angel often favours smoky abstracts and blurred colour. His inspirations can be equally ambiguous, emerging simply from a thought, a dream or a single moment in his day. At other times he can take a familiar theme and transform it into a print that evokes emotion rather than recognition. For Spring/Summer 2012, pyramid floor plans and illustrations of Cleopatra are transformed into an array of sunset colours. The fact that Egypt is his mother's home country gives the digital prints a personal connection that can only add to their sincerity.

"Digital print allows me to create whatever image I want and with as many colours and layers as I can imagine without restricting myself."
Michael Angel

LEFT Printed silk chiffon tunic shirt, Michael Angel, Spring/Summer 2009: Sheer chiffon plays over skin and lamé shorts. Using a characteristically abstract design, Angel places the print strategically across the shirt.

OPPOSITE Printed outfit, Michael Angel, Spring/Summer 2010: Created for his lookbook, this image by photographer Ryan Bertroche exemplifies Angel's strong, urban aesthetic.

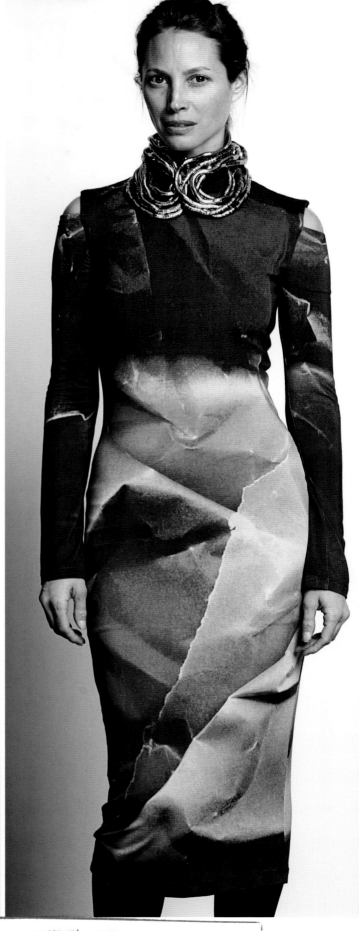

Michael Angel   27

PREVIOUS PAGES

Christy Turlington Burns wears
Autumn/Winter 2011–12 collection,
Michael Angel: Crumpled paper prints
are rendered across four outfits. The
array demonstrates the way in which
a single idea morphs and develops
across a variety of shapes and fabrics.

OPPOSITE

Crystal flowers
dress, Michael Angel, Spring/
Summer 2010: Vivid, jewel-like prints
are emblazoned across a sculpted
dress reminiscent of Dior's New Look
silhouette of 1947. Angel's sharp,
futuristic version nevertheless retains
a classic mood through his use of
cool black and an elegant wrapped
shawl collar.

RIGHT

Printed chiffon kaftan
and leggings, Michael Angel, Autumn/
Winter 2008–9: Smoky photographic
images recur throughout Michael
Angel's collections. They mirror the
sinuous fabrics and soft, indistinct
cuts of his looser pieces. Frequently
contrasted with solid colour, the prints
are always connected through his
sophisticated palette.

ABOVE Sketch, *Renaissance* collection, Michael Angel, Autumn/ Winter 2008: Ivory and black merino wool apron dress with printed silk charmeuse lining.

OPPOSITE Sketch, *Renaissance* collection, Michael Angel, Autumn/ Winter 2008–9: Printed charmeuse dress with wool detailing: "When sketching I always use the print as an overlay as it helps to dictate the print placement." *Michael Angel*

RIGHT Pixellated column dress, Michael Angel, Autumn/Winter 2008–9: Angel expands his print to reveal the colour pixels that comprise the design.

ABOVE Advertising image, *Renaissance* collection, Michael Angel, Autumn/Winter 2008–9: Printed silk chiffon *Pieta* dress with oversized hood from Angel's first runway collection.

ABOVE Peplum top, *Degas Behind Stained Glass* collection, Michael Angel, Autumn/Winter 2009–10: A printed nylon shell bonded to neoprene. "This was the first time I explored bonded fabric. We fused jersey to neoprene to create structure – it was about evolving what we could print." *Michael Angel*

Antoni & Alison

Since meeting at St Martin's School of Art in 1982, and working together as Antoni & Alison since 1987, Antoni Burakowski and Alison Roberts have always maintained a more "Art Studio" than "Fashion Studio" slant, insisting that "just because fashion is the way it is, doesn't mean it has to be the way it is."

In recent years, their renowned print work has embraced digital processes. Together they have always created highly individual pieces, and for Autumn/Winter 2012–13, the designers returned to the catwalk for the first time since 2005. They presented a series of simple silk shifts printed with photographs of magnified fabrics and trims. Playful and unique, the collection reflected Antoni & Alison's former work and took it to a new plane.

"Digital print didn't exist when we started Antoni & Alison and neither did mobile phones or everyday use of computers," says Burakowski. "To get a photographic image this had to be done by silk-screen printing using a four-screen CMYK process... These techniques proved incredibly costly, as you had to pay a fortune to open screens and then needed to order a huge amount of metreage to make the prints cost-effective."

The arrival of digital printing has solved a dilemma for the designers who have long wanted to work thoroughly and broadly with photographic images. "Working with photography had big limitations for us, silk-screen and litho-wise," says Burakowski. "We wanted to work a lot with photography from early on in a more fine art rather than a textile way." In this highly visual age, digital printing offers limitless scope for sampling and exploring pictures as a flat media.

After a few experiments, Burakowski and Roberts started working with digital print properly in 2003. "We've always pushed the boundaries and it [digital print] has so much potential that we really have only scratched the surface. It has solved many problems for us and made us think of even more. These days it has an accuracy so that you really can get what you visualize – which is amazing!"

"Digital print to us is like a new art form. We can do everything we ever wanted to do and more."
Burakowski & Roberts

ABOVE *D* collection, *Vim* print, Antoni & Alison, Spring/Summer 2004: "This print was for us the most complicated we could think of at the time. It broke all the rules that we had had to follow regarding silk screen printing." *Antoni Burakowski & Alison Roberts*

OVERLEAF Dresses, Autumn/Winter 2012–13; Spring/Summer 2013: "The dress shapes are perfect for what we need to do. The print has all of the structure in them – there really is no need for us to change the style each season." *Antoni Burakowski & Alison Roberts*

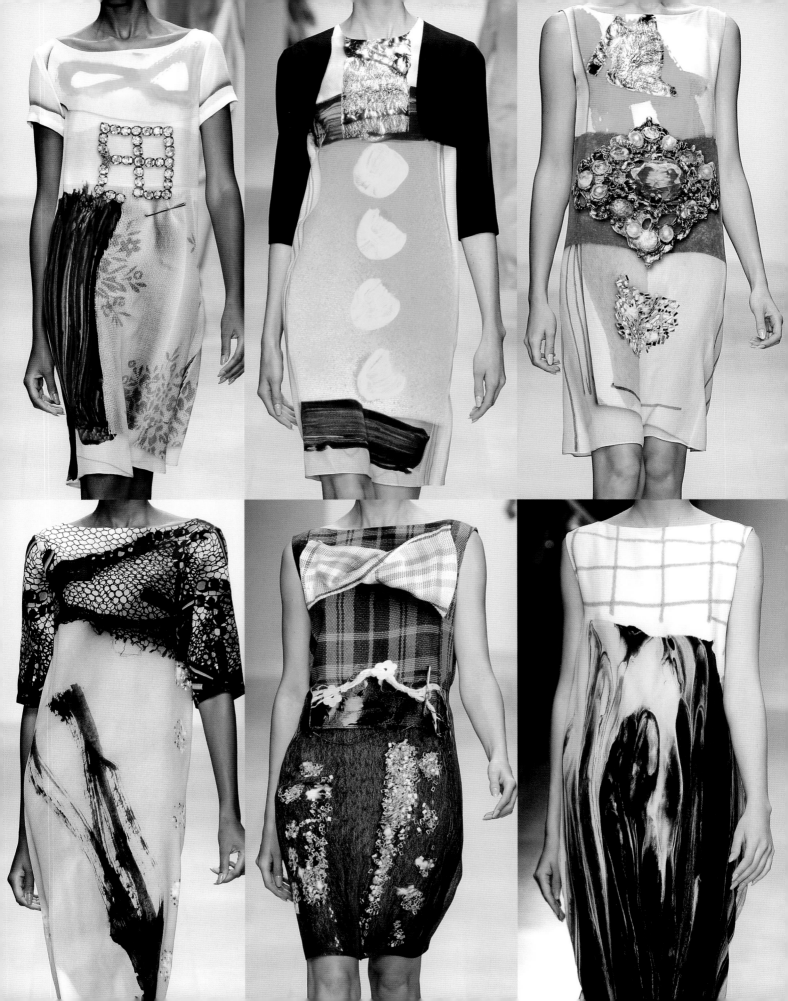

ABOVE Hessian and bow skirt, 2013: A silk crepe de Chine skirt, soft
and light to the touch, is printed with the roughly textured weave of hessian. The
photographic nature of the print makes this a playful, almost surreal conceit.

ABOVE Staples and glitter skirt, 2013: "The styles are specifically made to just 'put on and go' – just like blank pieces of paper they are completely transformed by their print." *Antoni Burakowski and Alison Roberts*

LEFT AND OPPOSITE

Antoni & Alison's silk crepe de Chine scarves (top left) *Purple Drawing* scarf; (below left) *Blue Drawing* scarf; (top right) *Brown Felt and Gems* scarf; (below right) *Red Sequins* scarf: "[With our scarves] the artwork is the most important thing thing to us. To us they are like souvenirs of our work and you can either wear them or collect them. The scarf is as close to a piece of paper as we can get." *Antoni Burakowski & Alison Roberts*

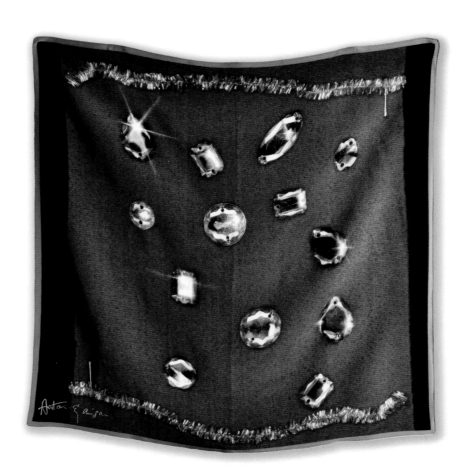

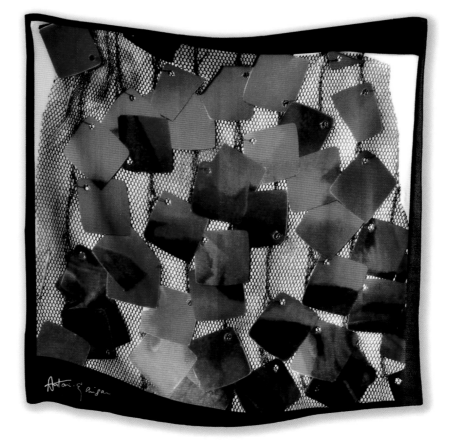

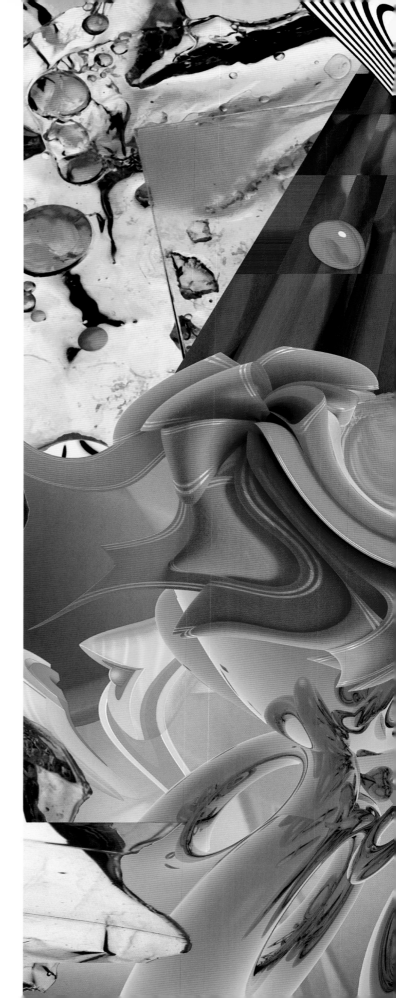

Basso & Brooke

Bruno Basso and Christopher Brooke are a partnership that could have been designed for digital-print textiles. Basso, born in São Paulo, Brazil, studied advertising and journalism at college, and from 1998 worked as a graphic designer and art director. Christopher Brooke, from Newark-on-Trent in the UK, studied fashion at both Kingston University and Central Saint Martins. Basso oversees the textile prints and Brooke creates the garments to which they are fused.

Together the pair launched their eponymous label Basso & Brooke in 2003, pioneering work in graphics-generated textile design. The partnership's approach was to apply print to every surface, in doing so creating a unique aesthetic. In 2004 it won them London's first Fashion Fringe Award, a prize created to support emerging fashion talent. According to Brooke, their energetic and original work was created to "confuse people, playing on aesthetics and people's idea of bad taste, but creating it in a way that they maybe don't realize the initial starting point."

Their vision was certainly bewildering, but Basso and Brooke earned wider recognition for their innovative work. Famously described as "the Pixar of clothes" by Tim Blanks of Style.com for their technological element, in 2009, US First Lady Michelle Obama chose to wear a piece from their Spring/Summer collection at a White House function.

Travel is an important part of the duo's modus operandi (Basso talks about collecting "emotional material" on his journeys). Prints emerge from their trips both as a record and as a physical response to experiences. In 2009, Basso and Brooke undertook a 10-day residency in Uzbekistan. While visiting Samarkand, Tashkent and Margilan in the Fergana Valley, they spent three days studying traditional ikat weaving. The resulting prints were displayed at the Design Museum, an honour rarely accorded to fashion designers.

As well as clothing, Basso & Brooke's prints have decorated a wide variety of products, from a tent to packaging for lipstick. The long-term potential of prints can add a fresh dimension to a brand's durability, as evidenced by Emilio Pucci and Hermès, both of which have long outlasted their creators, thanks in no small part to their signature textiles. Basso & Brooke may aspire to be their digital successors in the knowledge that they are one of the very first companies to attempt to do so.

RIGHT *Swan Lake* print, Basso & Brooke, Spring/Summer 2010: A bright and wild pattern brings together mismatched visual elements: abstracted snatches of Jeff Koons' *Balloon Dog* inflatable sculpture, bubbles suspended in coloured liquid and contrasting monochromes.

In the summer of 2006, Dorchester Hotels commissioned Basso & Brooke to create The Dorchester collection – outfits to represent their international properties.

RIGHT *The Beverly Hills Hotel, Los Angeles.* A voluptuous Hollywood premiere dress decorated with printed, sequined and beaded motifs and finished with a red carpet train.

OPPOSITE *The Dorchester, London.* A 1950s-inspired ball gown embellished with gold and white bugle beads and design motifs taken from the hotel's Oliver Messel Suite.

OVERLEAF Basso & Brooke has amassed an impressive archive of prints since its first collection in 2004. The label's many collaborations have included work with Converse and The Cambridge Satchel Company.

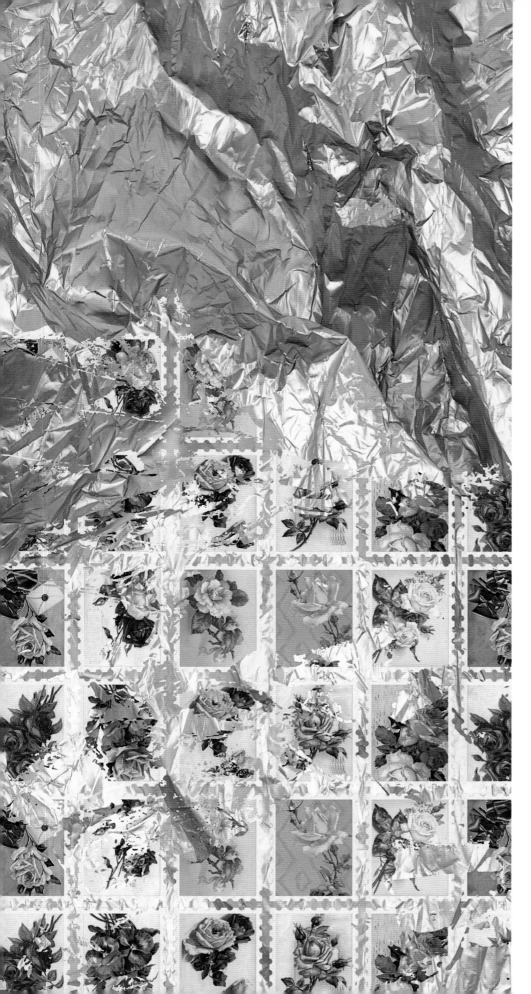

LEFT *Stamped Gold Crush* print, Basso & Brooke, Spring/Summer 2011: In a collection of prints that featured paper ephemera and vintage illustrations of flowers, the designers added dramatic ersatz texture by melding them with billowing gold foil. The flat nature of digital printing can be overcome with the shadow and highlights within photographic images.

OPPOSITE Coat and dress, Basso & Brooke, Spring/Summer 2011: A feminine and antique mood is achieved with layers of distressed prints and a softer palette.

OVERLEAF (left) *Art of Thrill*, Spring/Summer 2012. (right) *Nippon Pop*, Spring/Summer 2009.

Hussein Chalayan

Hussein Chalayan's designs are revered not only by the world of fashion but by the art establishment, too: the critic Andrew Graham-Dixon said: "His work is as close to contemporary art as you can get." The London-based designer's garments have been exhibited in museums and art galleries worldwide, a testament to his inventiveness and people's reactions to it. That he allows his garments to exist as precious *objets* in our highly commercial fashion environment has also marked him out as a maverick throughout his career since graduation from Central Saint Martins in 1993.

Hussein Chalayan is a fashion designer whose work emerges from rigorous and original thought. Because it can take him to uncharted regions of couture, at times he finds himself looking for solutions beyond the pattern-cutting table and dress stand. "Technology is the only way through which you can do new things... Technology allows you to create new combinations, new relationships, new interactions," he explained. It is that technology which helps him to overcome the usual limitations of fashion, and it's within this sphere that his results are most spectacular. They have included video dresses embedded with 15,000 LEDs to display video sequences across the entire surface of the dress (2007) and metal animatronic dresses that rapidly morphed through more than a century of silhouettes (2006).

The myriad effects that can be achieved with digital printing make it an ideal technique for a modernist. It features throughout Chalayan's work as creative director of Puma Black Label, where it lends a technical, modern edge to trainers and stretch garments. On his Conflate Graphic shoe he metamorphosed images of materials used on space vehicles into a tessellated floral print.

Chalayan's curiosity for discovering boundaries and then testing them extends across his work, from concept to presentations. Consequently, as with the more experimental designers, he employs programmers, engineers and producers to achieve his vision. His career has exactly spanned the emergence of digital technologies, his collections a timeline of investigations into how far they can transmit fashion into the future.

OPPOSITE *Inertia* collection, Hussein Chalayan, Spring/Summer 2009: Chalayan explored the speed of modern life through dresses printed with images of crushed motor vehicles and moulded in latex to appear as a freeze frame.

RIGHT Column dress, *Seize the Day* collection, Hussein Chalayan, Spring/Summer 2013: This finale dress was created as an elegant minimalist column divided into transparent silk chiffon and silk black marble print.

OVERLEAF Two-in-one dress, *Rise* collection, Hussein Chalayan, Autumn/Winter 2013–14: A dress mutates from cocktail to a full-length gown with a pull at the neckline, inspired by "the dichotomy between domestically earthbound environments: disembodiment and metamorphosis".

LEFT *Speed Flare* dress, Hussein Chalayan, Spring/Summer 2013: Chalayan blends sportswear with daywear in a luxurious dress with contrasting cuts of 3-D net and a printed cotton patchwork – a piece that represents the playful and wearable aspect of his work.

OPPOSITE Print dress, *Domisilent* collection, Autumn/Winter 2012–13: A graphic and subtle design inspired by "bacteria and ship parts" is printed onto a lithe sheath dress.

Tsumori Chisato

Unique prints are Tsumori Chisato's trademark. Born in the city of Saitama, Japan, Chisato studied fashion at the Bunka Fashion College in Tokyo, where her fellow alumni included Yohji Yamamoto, Junya Watanabe and Kenzo Takada. In 1977, she joined Issey Miyake to design his "Issey Sports", later renamed "I.S. Chisato Tsumori Design". After more than a decade with Miyake, Chisato started her own line in 1990, which was debuted in Tokyo at the Japan Fashion Week that same year.

Chisato has since found her fashion home in Paris, where her bold and vivid collections bring an original vision to the twice-yearly collections. Compared to the grand fashion houses that surround Chisato, her style is individual and whimsical. It rarely reflects commercial trends; instead it projects her distinctive viewpoint and her own personal style. Like many designers, she creates her collections for herself.

That style is also expressed through her prints. Sweeping strokes of bright, painted colour are often juxtaposed with bold solids. Cute, cartoony sketches in watercolours or coloured pens are uplifting and amusing – Chisato hopes that they convey a "bright and positive feeling" – and are taken from her own sketchbooks. The designer, who as a child wanted to be a manga illustrator, claims to draw "most of the time". Her style of hand-drawn, sketchy artwork makes digital printing an ideal option.

Tsumori Chisato is an international designer in every respect. She claims to feel neither French nor Japanese and her business is rooted in both countries (her office remains in Tokyo). Travel is at the heart of her design philosophy. After each show, Chisato begins her research for the next one with a trip to a country she has never before visited. There she explores the textiles, colours, local craft techniques and culture. She then combines her experiences with her own character and tastes to create a vision based on the journey. A trip to Switzerland with her husband inspired cable-car prints using photographic images; a way of "turning memories into prints". Carpets from Turkey, a glass vase from Syria... Chisato is a creative magpie, and her eclectic world-traveller style permeates every collection.

LEFT *Block Bird* silk dress, Tsumori Chisato, Spring/Summer 2012: Chisato's lighthearted side comes out through a print featuring cartoon Godzilla characters. For this collection the designer, whose travelogue is her inspiration, evoked Costa Rica, Cuba and Miami.

OPPOSITE Printed skirt and top, Tsumori Chisato, Autumn/Winter 2012–13. The hand-painted aesthetic favoured by Chisato offers an interesting alternative to perfect graphic prints created using Illustrator software.

LEFT Black silk strapless jumpsuit, Tsumori Chisato, Spring/Summer 2012: Hand-drawn blooms are arranged down the sides of the figure to frame and shape it, the matching parasol a characteristically cute touch by Chisato.

OPPOSITE LEFT Leopard print dress, Tsumori Chisato, Spring/Summer 2011: Cartoon leopards and loose squiggles are gathered on an airy dress for her twentieth anniversary collection.

OPPOSITE RIGHT Leopard and flower print dress, Tsumori Chisato, Spring/Summer 2011: A complex garment combines a multitude of prints and colours and vintage 1930s-style takes on a comedic quality.

OPPOSITE Printed Godzilla skirt, Tsumori Chisato, Spring/Summer 2012: A cast of cartoon characters painted by Chisato plays across a prehistoric backdrop. Through print the designer creates her own highly individual vision of contemporary fashion.

LEFT Backstage, Tsumori Chisato, Spring/Summer 2012: Kitsch and cute, models take on the mood of a Tsumori Chisato show. Naïve, hand-painted flowers explode across the front of the tunic dress, engineered to create a central focal point.

Clover Canyon

Clover Canyon is a label that reflects its location. Designed and produced in Los Angeles, the collection is named after Laurel Canyon, the Hollywood Hills neighbourhood associated with California's hippie culture. It creates streamlined clothes united with eclectic and individual prints. The design team, headed by creative director Rozae Nichols, begins the design process, "expressing the mood of a place, its historical textiles, of a time, old-world and new, with humour". A sense of collective optimism is expressed through the prints, and the active style of the team's digital sketches (see pages 66–7) conveys the pacy, energetic approach that drives it.

The content of the prints reflects a creative journey for the design team. Its use of engineered prints and bordered layouts is a constant. "I believe [they] can visually balance and redirect organic, neo-Baroque elements of contemporary design," explains Nichols. "Throughout the years, this has remained integral to our print composition and textile designs. Our use of borders and engineered layout is modern yet is approached with reverence to centuries of traditional textile and print compositions."

Although designing a print to fit within the physical boundaries of a garment is not an entirely new skill, digital printing multiplies a designer's options to create garments and prints as a single process. Print can now exist within the structure of a garment rather than simply decorating it. "The final styles reflect the thrilling moment when the garment's pattern pieces and our graphic art meld in synergy," explains Nichols.

The progression of digital printing maintains its momentum, she continues. "The ever advancing digital techniques can certainly expedite the print-art making process and create an intriguing, modern visual experience which was perhaps only dreamed of in past generations of textile print design." However, maintaining a respect for the time-honoured methods of printing is important to Clover Canyon: "My hope is that within our evolving modern aesthetic, creative makers and designers will strive to think critically and connect newest forms with the value of traditional visual symbols and avoid the temptation of immediately derived sterile, slick effects."

"Thoughtful content is so vital to authentic design." Rozae Nichols

LEFT *Turquoise Valley* jacket, shirt and trousers, Clover Canyon, 2013: Vivid florals pop across the entire outfit and contrast with the narrow shawl collar, button and cuffs.

OPPOSITE LEFT Ombré paisley sequin jacket and ombré paisley trousers, Clover Canyon, Autumn/Winter 2012–13: A dramatic pairing combines a sequined surface on the jacket and amber tones graduated up the trouser legs.

OPPOSITE RIGHT *Orchid Garden* velvet dress, Clover Canyon, Autumn/Winter 2012–13: A classic jersey dress cut from silk and cotton velvet is saturated with vibrant digitized orchids.

OPPOSITE LEFT *Peacock* tunic, Clover Canyon, Pre-Autumn 2013: A sheer tunic is bordered with a geometric pattern to create a square frame for an expansive peacock print.

OPPOSITE RIGHT Tunic and trousers, Clover Canyon, Pre-Autumn 2013: A loose tunic and trouser combination can create a spectacular play between prints. The front hem is shortened to reveal the coordinating print below.

RIGHT *Miami Streets* jacket and shorts, Clover Canyon, Resort 2012: Gathered shorts and a relaxed jacket are cut from a washed crepe decorated with the symbols and mood of Miami life.

Giles Deacon

"Democracy of fashion" is British designer Giles Deacon's declared goal. To achieve his aim he works across the fashion business and beyond. His catwalk collections are so well crafted and expensive that they stop just short of haute couture (he uses machines rather than the required hand-work to create them), yet he has relished his high-street collaborations and the chance to sell his jewellery range on a shopping channel. He has illustrated a wrap for the iconic British telephone kiosk, designed in 1936, and even designed a dress for the Cadbury chocolate bunny. In short, Deacon has tapped every opportunity to connect with his audience rather than keep it at arm's length.

Deacon has a playful, slightly subversive, attitude toward fashion. For his inspirations he embraces the full range of modern culture, both high and low. He also uses the full range of fashion techniques to express them, usually with a twist: his T-shirts might be decorated with elegant demi-couture embroidery and his grand evening gowns printed with ultra-modern photo print images. He is a pragmatist, however. Deacon's made-to-measure dresses can cost up to £20,000 ($30,000); the woman who can afford that sort of price tag is likely to allow her sense of humour only so much free reign.

Deacon was brought up in the Lake District, an idyllic and remote region of England. After a brief flirtation with marine biology, he chose instead to attend art college, finishing at Central Saint Martins in London. On graduation, he worked with Jean-Charles de Castelbajac, the French designer known for his good-humoured, print-heavy collections.

Deacon has sketched and drawn his way through life, unlike a surprising number of designers. It's one of the things that strongly connects him to his print work. His own sketches and doodles appear through his prints, some created on an iPad. These cartoon influences often creep onto Deacon's catwalk, and are used at times to add satire to an otherwise solemn section within a catwalk collection.

The inspiration may be his, but Deacon works with print specialists to create the designs. Sitting at a computer, they will scan images, alter them, print them out and repeat the process until the results are exactly as they need to be. Even when a print appears to be breezy and loose, it may have taken a considerable time to perfect.

LEFT Satin cocktail gown, Giles Deacon, Spring/Summer 2012: The modern, sharp and elegant print is softened with tinted feathers in a nod to the design itself.

OPPOSITE Backstage, Giles Deacon, Spring/Summer 2012: Deacon arrived at his swan theme via the society glamour of Cecil Beaton and the sharp modernity of Andy Warhol's Factory. His uncompromising use of the dramatic prints reveals the fierce, combative nature of the bird.

OVERLEAF (left to right) Autumn/Winter 2013–14; Autumn/Winter 2011–12; Spring /Summer 2009; Autumn/Winter 2005–6.

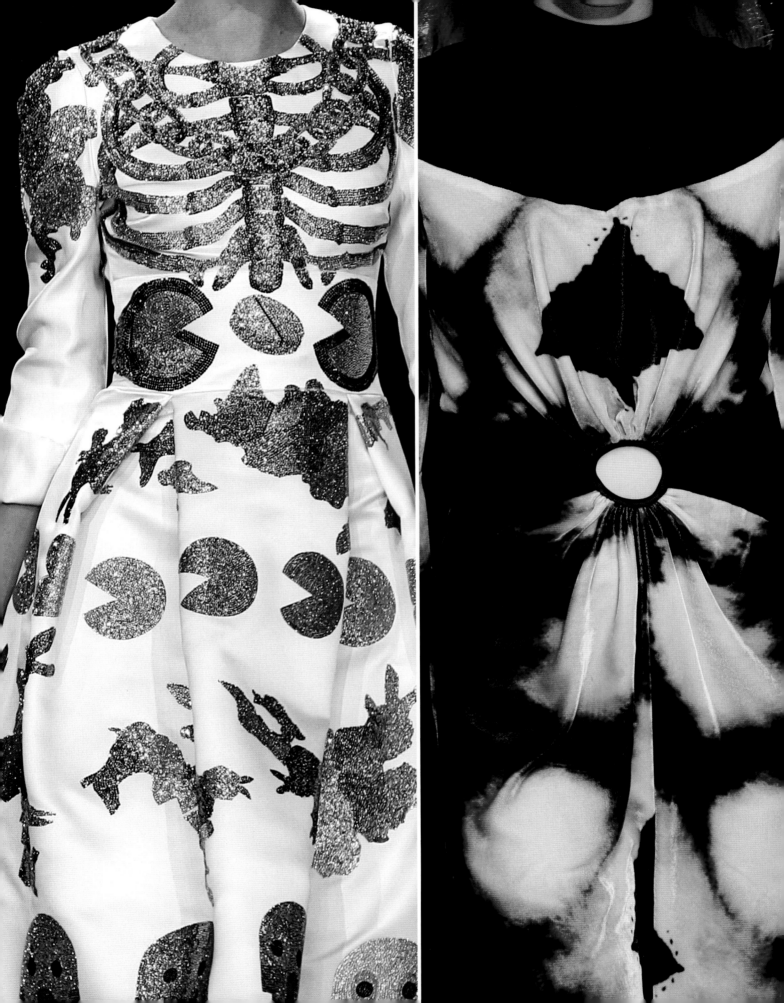

RIGHT *Untitled*, Giles Deacon and Jeremy Deller, 2012: As part of the London 2012 Festival, British fashion designers and visual artists collaborated on a series of works. Here, Deacon and conceptual artist Deller created a full-body running suit with cape, staff of wood and leather, and a hat decorated with dark brown satin leaves and black burnt peacock feathers on a black felt hat base.

Dolce & Gabbana

Dolce & Gabbana is a powerhouse of Italian fashion. Known for its romantic, Mediterranean look, the house style spans the many collections now created under the Dolce & Gabbana umbrella. Palermo-born Domenico Dolce and Venice-born Stefano Gabbana met in the early 1980s when both worked in a small atelier. Six years later, the pair launched their own collection, one that has grown to become one of Italy's largest fashion houses. One of the defining reasons for its success has been its youthful takes on the cultural traditions of Dolce's Sicilian roots combined with the elegantly fantastical impression of Italy created by film director Federico Fellini in the 1950s and '60s. They have emerged as black tailoring for men and women, sultry leopard prints, lingerie-inspired dresses and deep fronds of heavy lace borrowed from Catholic regalia.

Dolce & Gabbana's devotion to *La Bella Figura* – the Italian desire for splendid presentation through art and personal appearance – is reflected throughout their prints. It can evoke any aspect of their universe, from the atmosphere of a Baroque palazzo to the famous puppets of Sicilian street theatres. At the core of these themes is an extravagance of colour and detail. It also uses a degree of facsimile or photographic work that is ideal for rendering using the digital printing processes.

The frenetic mix-and-match aesthetic employed by Dolce & Gabbana signifies a restlessness in their personal approach to work. Change and progression continue to drive their business as the designers work toward their thirtieth anniversary. Their fascination for current affairs and digital culture means they were the first designer house to invite fashion bloggers to sit front row at their Spring/Summer show in 2009 and live-stream their show in 2005. Balancing their trusted traditions with leading-edge technology has become a specialty.

It enables them to maintain a strong and individual visual identity. For Spring/Summer 2013, Dolce & Gabbana returned to its roots with a collection that focused on Sicily and its folk culture. 1960s-inspired tourist prints decorated the briefest of miniskirts as well as a series of tunics worn with trousers and shorts. Unapologetically retro spirit and modern in their complex palette, they bring together the old and the new.

LEFT Backstage, Dolce & Gabbana, Spring/Summer 2013: Model Bette Franke is transformed into Dolce & Gabbana's fantasy tourist on a trip around the sights of Sicily.

OPPOSITE Backstage, Dolce & Gabbana, Spring/Summer 2013: Colourful and playful beach outfits inspired by 1950s Italian resortwear.

OVERLEAF Dolce & Gabbana, Spring/Summer 2013; Autumn/Winter 2013–14; Autumn/Winter 2012–13: Dolce & Gabbana's textile work is a major part of their storytelling, and print remains one of the designers' strong signatures. Their inspirations emerge in prints that include battle scenes, medieval knights and floral vignettes (Spring/Summer 2013, left); Byzantine mosaics in the famous Monreale Cathedral, Sicily (Autumn/Winter 2013–14, top right); and "Romantic Baroque" paintings from Sicilian palazzi (Autumn/Winter 2012–13, bottom right).

ABOVE Menswear collection, Dolce & Gabbana, Autumn/ Winter 2013–14: For their show, 82 men were cast from villages in the Sicilian countryside. The designers celebrated their Catholic devotion through a series of sweatshirts bearing religious symbols and icons.

OPPOSITE Printed shirt and shorts, Dolce & Gabbana, Autumn/Winter 2012–13: A kitsch collision of painting and needlepoint prints creates an arresting outfit. The sporty and modest garment shapes add to the designers' counterpoint approach.

Fabitoria

Taiwanese label Fabitoria is a collaboration between Fabiana Chang and Victoria Kao. Both were born in 1989 and majored in fashion design at Taipei's Shih Chien University. Chang has also worked as a graphic designer. Post-modernism and Surrealism are central themes of Fabitoria. "We break free from conventional thoughts and frames, and in a way, reform the world through digital print," explains Kao. The pair use only digital print in their work because for them traditional printing is incapable of reproducing the wide range of colours and three-dimensional effects they seek.

To date, Fabitoria's collections have focused on skirts. By limiting their vision, they are better able to develop their label at a manageable pace. For their first season, in 2012, Fabitoria released 12 different skirts that used unrelated details. "Fabiana and I are two girls who are a little bit alike and a little bit different," says Kao. "We are each fascinated by the way the other sees the world." A skirt for them offers the same versatility of viewpoint: "When different types of girls wear the same skirt, they give off entirely different vibes."

Kao and Chang begin each season talking through the main ideas and elements of focus. Afterwards they create prototypes and discuss any changes to be made. Chang then works on the digital files for the prints, combining different images and colour combinations. When this is done, they finalize the designs together by finding a balance between their viewpoints.

Fabitoria exemplifies a youthful and unreserved approach to the digital process. The partnership also exists because of digital printing since it's the primary element of their work. As Keo explains, "Compared to other media within textiles, digital printing is for us the technique that is capable of most directly and profoundly evoking reactions in people's hearts. If digital printing had not existed, I suppose we could never have started, or our path may have been completely different."

> *"It would have been much more difficult to consolidate our ideas without digital printing."*
> Victoria Kao

LEFT Fabitoria skirts are designed to be worn either way round; the pockets feature the main print and are placed against a solid colour to create a focus for the design. "This print is the familiar Queen Elizabeth I. Because digital printing is capable of fine detail, we can present all the details of the design – the queen can even playfully put on a pair of rose-coloured glasses." (see also pages 88–9) *Victoria Kao & Fabiana Chang*

OPPOSITE, ABOVE AND BELOW "This picture was taken from the Maokong Gondola in Taipei. It's a place where people often visit for its famous tea and scenic views. It's also the place where Fabiana grew up. We added a dragonfly that appears to be standing on the camera lens to give it an extra sense of liveliness. The centrally placed line of the dragonfly on the skirt is also a way of secretly looking slimmer than you actually are." *Victoria Kao & Fabiana Chang*

OPPOSITE "This is my own fish tank," explains Kao. "If you look closely, you can even see some shrimp. We've combined the fish tank with sapphires – the material of the textile for printing is very important for reproducing the desired colours."

RIGHT *Porcelain Ceremony* skirt, Spring/Summer 2013: Delicate porcelain bowls are printed across a handmade skirt.

OVERLEAF "Combining Surrealism and Post-Impressionism with our instinctive sense of colour combinations through digital techniques, each one of our designs is its own work of art. If digital printing had not existed, I suppose we could never have started, or our path may have been completely different."
Victoria Kao & Fabiana Chang

FABITORIA

Holly Fulton

Holly Fulton creates unique and complicated prints. So strong is her signature that she is sometimes mistaken for a textiles designer, but her collections are a clear marriage of print and construction.

Like many of the London-based fashion designers who have embraced digital printing, Fulton draws the designs herself. They emerge as hand-rendered, digitally manipulated patterns that draw on Art Deco lines and Bauhaus contours. She adds to the mix pop art themes, psychedelic illustrations and a dash of Gianni Versace's maximal prints from the early 1990s. Fulton's tangle of references are tamed by the simplicity of her garments. Luxurious and easy to wear, the shapes are sporty and minimal – ideal for her wealthy international clientele. The decoration may be lavish and original but these pieces are designed to sell.

Born in Scotland, Fulton studied fashion textiles at Edinburgh College of Art and the Royal College of Art. After working for Alber Elbaz at Lanvin, she established her own label in 2009. Her debut was at London's Fashion East, the non-profit initiative established by the Old Truman Brewery in 2000 to nurture emerging young designers.

"A digitally printed, full-length monochrome dress in silk jersey" is how Fulton characterizes her signature piece. She is also known for creating her own jewellery, something her mother did before her. In fact Fulton creates the jewellery at the same time as she does the clothes, and some pieces are designed to meld with her garments. Laser-cut Perspex, leather and architectural crystals are mixed with industrial elements such as hinges to make her eccentric and opulent accessories. As with her mechanical prints, this combination of the glamorous and the machined is a recurring feature of Fulton's work.

Fulton regards her work as being a contemporary update on couture techniques. Her mechanized print decoration contrasts with laboriously handcrafted details and unexpected materials. It is all underpinned with extensive research. For Holly Fulton, the entire process is a labour of love: "I always look to inspiration that I love and believe in my work – I have to love it as it takes quite a long time to make."

OPPOSITE Dungaree dress and shirt, Holly Fulton, Autumn/Winter 2013–14: Lipsticks are manipulated to become a Deco-inspired column and border on Fulton's dress. The theme is driven home with the model's bright red lips.

RIGHT Jacket and skirt, Holly Fulton, Autumn/Winter 2013–14: Cubes reminiscent of M C Escher's drawings are printed and patched into leather skirts.

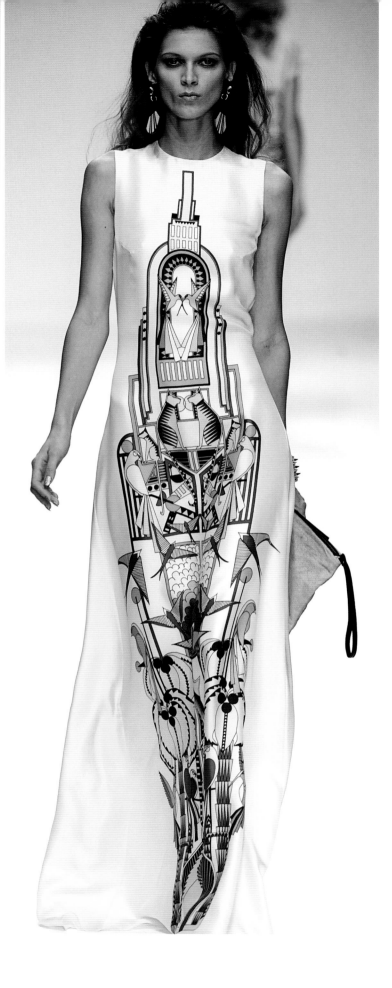

OPPOSITE Dungaree
dress and A-line tank gown, Holly
Fulton, Spring/Summer 2011: Fulton's
dungaree dress print is given a
geometric, almost African treatment
– intricate, unique and dramatic. The
curved corners and streamline stripes
or flutings of 1930s Odeon style run
the length of the gown.

RIGHT Backstage, Holly Fulton,
Spring/Summer 2012: Animal prints
and sharp, geometric shapes combine
in vivid contrast across Fulton's outfits.

LEFT Holly Fulton, Autumn/
Winter 2012: Hot-house blooms and
Deco motifs blend to create a design
for a cocktail dress. The resulting
"cage" is placed to encircle the hips
and create a form-lengthening effect.

OPPOSITE Printed yellow
and black top and trousers, Holly
Fulton, Spring/Summer 2012:
Yellow and black, nature's own
danger warning, presents a bold
fashion message. The designer
chose to open her show with this
duo, applied as chequerboard
squares and a placement print at
the hem of her trousers.

Givenchy

Riccardo Tisci's vision for Givenchy is both intensely modern and varied. Through digital print he has travelled from light, tropical flowers for his birds-of-paradise prints for Spring/Summer 2012 menswear to a sweatshirt emblazoned with a deconstructed Bambi, moody in both attitude and hue, featured in his Autumn/Winter 2013–14 womenswear show.

Dark drama is currently at the heart of a modern Givenchy collection. The French fashion house, once renowned for dressing Audrey Hepburn and Jacqueline Kennedy Onassis, has been brought to street level by Riccardo Tisci. He is part of an important new collective of designers who have injected rock-and-roll attitude into haute couture. In doing so, they have given new relevance to the exquisite techniques and standards associated with couture. On the surface, Tisci's style is a world away from that of Hubert de Givenchy, the house's aristocratic founder. What he does bring to the label is his Gothic version of romance. He regards darkness as beautiful, something that cues up his reputation for creating urban haute couture with a sharp edge.

Tisci was raised in Como, traditionally the home of Italy's world-renowned silk manufacturers. Trained at Central Saint Martins in London, he spent a brief period producing his own collections before he was appointed as creative director at Givenchy in 2005 to oversee haute couture, ready-to-wear and accessories. Just as John Galliano embraced the challenge at Christian Dior and succeeded, Tisci has managed to grow the haute couture business at the same time as creating a thriving ready-to-wear line.

Tisci's prints reflect his picante taste. They explore a variety of themes through the use of photographic imagery and the manipulation of graphic images into geometric patterns. For Tisci's menswear in particular, the spikiness of his eye-catching motifs – Rottweiler dogs, military jet themes and sharks – are obvious and tread a fine balance between kitsch and cool. They also reflect more profound, challenging themes. Tisci, a Catholic, is deeply religious. His Autumn/Winter 2011–12 menswear collection featured images of the Madonna subverted from Renaissance paintings. Nothing, it seems, is sacred for him when it comes to creating his signature printed T-shirts and sweatshirts.

LEFT Satin skirt and printed-sleeve top, Givenchy, Autumn/Winter 2011–12: Dark, sophisticated and dramatic, Riccardo Tisci's outfit uses engineered print as a foil to the sheer organza bodice that leaves the model exposed.

OPPOSITE Satin and organza dress, Givenchy, Autumn/Winter 2011–12: Moth-like blooms barely soften the dark borders that edge the main body of the dress, which features sheer fabric to lighten the hem.

LEFT Actress Liv Tyler, a spokesperson for Givenchy, wears an outfit that was shown on the menswear catwalk Spring/Summer 2012 collection. Tisci enjoys gender play throughout his fashion work and regularly shows womenswear within his men's collections.

OPPOSITE LEFT
Jacket and shorts, Givenchy, Spring/Summer 2012: The same spectacular tropical-bloom print was used across the men's collection, here applied to a summer suit.

OPPOSITE RIGHT
T-shirt and skirt, Givenchy, Spring/Summer 2012: Tisci shows his unorthodox side with a printed cotton skirt for men.

Josh Goot

Since his label's launch at Australian Fashion Week in 2005, Josh Goot has developed his own "optimistic, sporty, minimal" signature. His collections are bold, bright and modern, with some outfits reminiscent of a contemporary canvas. As a child growing up in Sydney, Australia, Goot was exposed to music and the visual arts, the latter of which is directly reflected in his work. "I'm artistic but I don't really see myself as an artist," he says. Instead, Goot regards himself as a disciplined and restrained creative. The label, in turn, reflects his home city's urban and professional style – as well as its sunny climate.

Goot's collections often feature prints juxtaposed with clean lines. The active nature of digital print can make the combination explosive. "Block colours can 'pop' elements of the print design, and negative space gives the print design room to breathe," says Goot. This contrasting play of light and shade, colour and monochrome, is one of the strongest features of his work.

He begins each collection with a theme or idea. "They often emerge from the natural world. Something that we all have a visual or experiential association with, that maybe we can look at in another way through digital print design and garment application." Working with the Sydney-based art director Shane Sakkeus, Goot blends his architectural shapes with their striking prints. Sometimes the construction follows, sometimes it leads. "It depends on the season. The ideas can evolve separately or together. In some cases, the print design and the garment come together at the very last moment. In other cases, they are conceived as one from the outset."

Although he is known for his powerful use of digital print, Goot doesn't introduce it to a collection unless it has a clear role. "An interest in digital print design can exist to the exclusion of other techniques," he explains. "As the seasons progress, we try to balance the digital art statement with other ideas in the collection to broaden the message, and make the whole story more interesting."

"The possibilities of digital print against clean lines make for a graphic contrast." Josh Goot

OPPOSITE Painted dress, Josh Goot, Spring/Summer 2011: Bold painted brush marks are drawn down a simple white gown.

LEFT *Water* print, Josh Goot and Shane Sakkeus, Spring/Summer 2009: "This art created the opening statement of our SS09 collection. To me, it conjures the feeling of diving into the ocean." *Josh Goot*

ABOVE

Flower Brocade print, Josh Goot and Shane Sakkeus, Spring/Summer 2012: "The hyper-real, photographic capture of roses and orchids has become a signature for the label. The flowers are composed with an ornamental frame. During the process, a Christmas beetle flew into [art director] Shane's house. It can be seen on a leaf in the print." *Josh Goot*

OPPOSITE LEFT

Vest and skirt, Josh Goot, L'Oréal Melbourne Fashion Festival 2009: Goot strips back the base of his photographic print to the simplest of garments to minimize confusion and direct focus to the image.

OPPOSITE RIGHT

Quake print, Josh Goot and Shane Sakkeus, Autumn/Winter 2010–11: "To me, it has a distinctly Australian feel. It reminds me of earth, opals and clouds." *Josh Goot*

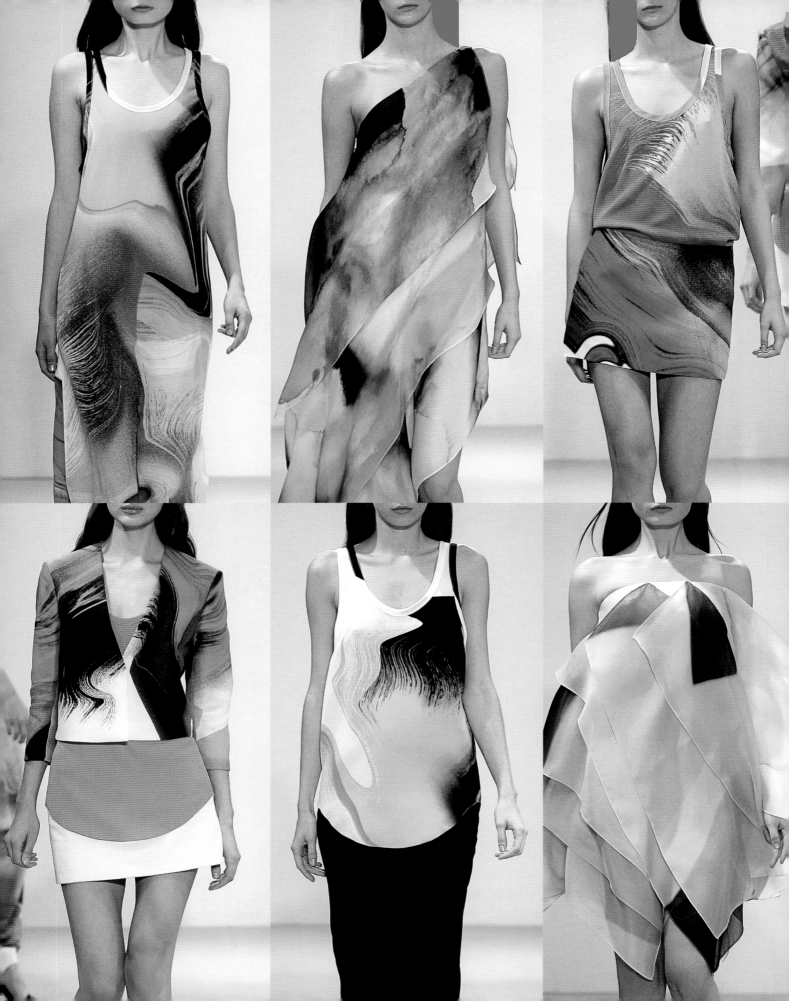

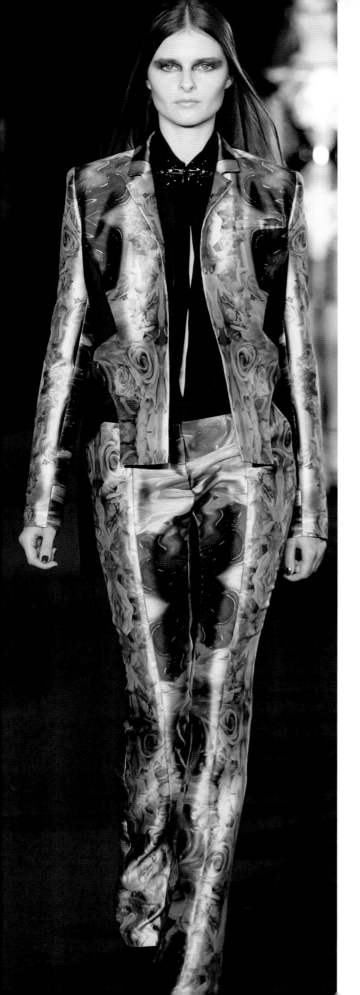

Prabal Gurung

Born in Singapore and raised in Kathmandu, Nepal, Gurung studied in New Delhi before taking a place at Parsons The New School for Design in New York. He went on to work as design director at Bill Blass before starting his own collection in 2009 with the words, "I just want to do beautiful, well-made clothes." Gurung's work epitomizes the New York tradition for luxurious, yet uncomplicated design. Whereas some designers wield their digital prints as a challenge to our prevailing perception of good taste, Gurung uses them to lightly spice his modern clothes.

The simplicity of this approach provides a masterclass for younger designers. Anyone looking to incorporate print into a wide and balanced collection would do well to observe how Gurung carefully edits and commits his use of it. His Resort 2013 collection was inspired by the work of Canadian artist Aaron Moran, a contemporary artist from British Columbia. Known for his abstract geometric sculptures created from found objects, Gurung reflected Moran's work through sharply cut garments married with digital, abstract prints. The artist's multi-tetrahedral wooden forms became kaleidoscopic prints with a three-dimensional twist. Most of the collection remained minimal: structured dresses and separates that used colour-blocking and sharp contrasts to reflect the theme. Where the print was used it was done so sparingly, and by ranging those prints across minimal shifts and skirts, they made the most impact.

Prabal Gurung's "guru" is the late Yves Saint Laurent. Just as his idol attracted a legion of famous, beautiful women to his label, Gurung has won many celebrity clients. In fact the actress Demi Moore cemented his career when she tweeted: "This is a new designer to look out for – Prabal Gurung." After seeing dresses from his first show, a small-scale, budget affair, Moore recognized Gurung's potential for creating red carpet stars. Maintaining a celebrity following is an important part of a contemporary designer's job, and keeping this choosy coterie happy largely depends on making them outfits that win the most column inches. It's no coincidence that Gurung's most noteworthy successes have included printed dresses worn by Michelle Obama and the Duchess of Cambridge. Print has the power to draw the eye and create a story for the caption writers, an advantage in our highly visual, online world.

LEFT *Sistine Blue Rose* print suit, Prabal Gurung, Autumn/Winter 2012–13: Shine is a regular theme for Gurung. An abstracted rose print is fused with iridescent fabric to create a glamorous yet futuristic trouser suit for his *Uncursed* collection.

OPPOSITE Backstage, Prabal Gurung, Spring/Summer 2012: The sweeps and curves of Gurung's prints are mirrored in the Linda Farrow butterfly sunglasses worn by the models. Spectacular paint effects are used on organza and latex to deepen a collection inspired by the artist and photographer Nobuyoshi Araki.

OPPOSITE AND
RIGHT Two dresses, Prabal
Gurung, Resort 2013: For his Resort
collection, Gurung employed the
work of Aaron Moran, a contemporary
artist from British Columbia known
for his abstract geometric sculptures
created from found objects. Gurung's
digital prints and Moran's independent
work both use sharp, precise lines
and elements found in nature, such
as wood grain.

RIGHT Turquoise *Painterly Lily*
sheath dress, Prabal Gurung, Pre-
Autumn 2013: The plainest silk and
cotton sateen dress is the backdrop
for a profusion of blooms – both
dramatic and simple.

OPPOSITE Apple green
and white *Painterly Lily* printed dress,
Prabal Gurung, Pre-Autumn 2013. A
silk and cotton strapless bustier dress
is given the option of an organza
double-hem for a striking fashion twist.

Christopher Kane

Occasionally a new designer arrives on the catwalk fully formed. The process of creating mature, polished collections takes most designers several seasons to achieve but Christopher Kane was one of those rare designers who launched with an energetic, edgy and saleable vision. His debut show in 2006 comprised body-con, neon bandage dresses that were summed up by the *International Herald Tribune*'s Suzy Menkes as "Imagine Marie Antoinette off to the disco in a concoction of lace, frothing like champagne... her stretch dress is as curvy as a corset and in neon bright colour. Absolutely fabulous!"

An elegantly pitched level of controversy underpins Kane's reputation. He often combines feminine, polite garments with provocative elements, a combination that appeals to both conservative and intrepid dressers. His prints frequently shock and awe even though they usually decorate the simplest or most ladylike garment. Frankenstein's monster, which made an appearance in Kane's Spring/Summer 2013 collection, atomic mushroom clouds, used in 2010, and his widely copied *Galaxy* prints, created for Resort 2011, are examples of how Kane has used digital printing to create those surprises. Images of far-flung nebulae taken through the Hubble telescope may be an expansive yet palatable motif, but more challenging are his "sinister but beautiful" nuclear explosions.

Born in Scotland, Kane studied at Central Saint Martins in London for six years. He worked with designers Giles Deacon and Russell Sage before setting up his own label on graduation. There is a collaborative element to Kane's success, however. Tammy Kane, his sister, muse and business partner, completed her own degree at the prestigious Scottish College of Textiles, and her experience is present across his collections. The label, known for testing the boundaries of textiles innovation, has been influential in its experimentations with maximal detail: glitter, embellished leather, lace and injection-moulded rubber, to name but a few. Kane never stands still; he restlessly moves through ideas each season without losing his signature.

Donatella Versace recognized this as an attribute shared with her late brother Gianni, and in 2009 she hired Kane to reinvigorate Versace's sister label, Versus. Kane used photo prints, on one occasion from the archives of photographer Bruce Weber, to create youthful T-shirts that put Versus back in the spotlight for a younger generation. His skill lies in knowing when to push the boundaries of print and when to let a simple idea breathe.

LEFT TV presenter Alexa Chung wears a leather *Galaxy* print dress by Christopher Kane, 2011. The now iconic prints created by Kane became a red carpet staple for women who appreciated their arresting but elegant impact.

OPPOSITE *Frankenstein* T-shirt, Christopher Kane, Spring/Summer 2013: Boris Karloff as Frankenstein is an unlikely motif but Kane translates the horror into high fashion by printing the character in hot, startling colour. With his dramatic, seasonal cotton tee, Kane makes a big statement against the simplest backdrop.

OPPOSITE LEFT Print and neon dress, Christopher Kane, Spring/Summer 2011: Yakuza tattoos worn by Japanese gangsters were the inspiration for the prints in an otherwise ladylike collection that also quoted the influence of the British Queen's late couturier, Norman Hartnell.

OPPOSITE RIGHT Print and neon dress, Christopher Kane, Spring/Summer 2011: A twinset and modest skirt are made modern with Kane's prints. The outfit and print are highlighted with neon flashes, a Kane signature.

RIGHT Satin tunic, Christopher Kane, Autumn/Winter 2013–14: Kane is no stranger to unusual springboards when it comes to ideas, and here he uses MRI scan images of a brain. The resulting magnetic fields and radio waves are intensely coloured and manipulated to create a yoke of abstract pattern.

RIGHT AND OPPOSITE *Galaxy* prints, Christopher Kane, Resort 2011: A digital print that captures a fashion mood can quickly become a trend in its own right. Christopher Kane achieved this and spawned a thousand imitators as well as creating myriad spin-offs, including a wrap design for a London taxi. His original collection best exemplifies the idea, however, with simple garments to showcase the deep, glorious hues added to the Hubble telescope's images of a trillion mile-long pillars of gas and nebulae.

Jen Kao

Los Angeles-born Jen Kao applies a rigorously modern and professional approach to every aspect of her business. On the catwalk it shows, although her tastes and experiences are more eclectic than her often pared-down clothes would suggest.

Raised in Kansas, Kao developed a taste for vintage style. She eventually moved to New York to study ceramic sculpture and creative writing before turning to fashion. Her decision to work from New York is a conscious one. Kao regards her design style as a natural fit for a fashion capital that is founded on contemporary, wearable luxury.

Kao is also known for looking to the realms of science for her contemporary edge. Her visuals in particular reference scientific themes: one satin print is inspired by NASA images of Earth from above and she cites Instagram's top media brand the *National Geographic* as her favourite website. Her father, Dr Min Kao, is credited with the breakthrough design and engineering of GPS software technology. She ascribes this aspect of her background as an influence on her fabric choices. Technical materials, neoprene and glow-in-the-dark finishes have all featured since the launch of her eponymous label in 2007.

Kao approaches each collection as a single process, preferring to keep much of the labour in-house. Her studio is a hive of experimentation as the garments emerge and she has established herself as a designer who merges the methodical aspects of her work with a love of contemporary culture. A fan of comic books, miniature Japanese food and video games, Kao is a natural collector whose references are drawn from across the widest spectrum.

Her precise tailoring and fluid draping are achieved through fabric manipulation and relentless sampling. Creative layering and crafted details give Kao's clothing a part cocktail, part casual style that transcends seasons and defined purposes. She looks to a future when the predominance of trends retreats and there is a renewed appreciation for individuality. Unsurprisingly, her fashion inspirations include Dries Van Noten and Tsumori Chisato, both designers known for the same approach, as well as highly personal print work.

LEFT Silk satin shirt dress, Jen Kao, Spring/Summer 2012: A vivid, multi-coloured print inspired by tropical blooms is broken up with patch pockets and waist detailing.

OPPOSITE Fringed multi-print dress, Jen Kao, Spring/Summer 2011: "A color palette of acid rainbows: Plush greens reinvent teals and blues... Touches of thermal yellows and nuclear oranges are borderline toxic, while muddy greys and inks create a landscape for a fiery-hued spectrum. All in rich silks, jerseys, metallics, fancy tweeds, and shape-shifting leathers." *Jen Kao*

LEFT Printed minidress and leggings, Jen Kao, Spring/Summer 2011: Solid colour is used across the top of the dress to give the outfit a depth it would otherwise lack.

OPPOSITE Fringed multi-print dress, Jen Kao, Spring/Summer 2011: The addition of fringing puts texture back into the outfit created from flat fabric. A complicated surface pattern is pushed further by this three-dimensional adjunct.

OPPOSITE Printed shirt dress, Jen Kao, Spring/Summer 2012: Taking inspiration from Baz Luhrmann's 1996 film *Romeo + Juliet*, Kao created a series of rosy, psychedelic prints morphing from florals to checks to ombré shadows.

RIGHT Printed bolero and dress, Jen Kao, Spring/Summer 2012: A soft, ruffled skirt is finished with a graphic border. The abbreviated jacket balances and contrasts with the peachy tones below.

Mary Katrantzou

Mary Katrantzou is a fashion designer of her time. The fact that she came to the catwalk during the digital print age was propitious for someone whose primary focus was textiles rather than garment construction. It enabled her to explore and develop a side to her talent that might otherwise have remained dormant.

Born in Athens, Katrantzou moved to the United States in 2003 to attend the Rhode Island School of Design to study architecture. She later attended Central Saint Martins in London to study textile and then fashion design. It wasn't until she was studying alongside fashion designers – all of whom were planning solo careers – that it occurred to Katrantzou that she should create her own label. Inspired by designers including Pierre Cardin and Yohji Yamamoto, she transformed herself into a fully fledged fashion designer.

Katrantzou went on to open the Central Saint Martins MA graduation show in 2008. Trompe l'oeil prints of oversized jewellery decorated jersey bonded dresses, creating the illusion of vast neckpieces. Katrantzou has since returned to photo-graphics with perfume bottles, artisan blown glass and eighteenth-century society paintings, while keeping the printed image central to her aesthetic.

It was as a student that Katrantzou was first recognized as a superb colourist. Her reputation was cemented, however, with her Autumn/Winter 2011–12 show. Remembered as her "Chinese lampshade" collection, it was an array of luminous, interiors-themed prints committed to silhouettes inspired by lampshades. It was a daring but successful gambit: 24 women were rumoured to have invested in Katrantzou's startling skirts, the most unlikely yet precious buy of that particular season. For Autumn/Winter 2013–14, Katrantzou removed the colour to produce a tonal range. Her intention was to refocus on the garment within rather than the surface design, although her digital prints remained an integral part of the collection.

As much as Mary Katrantzou has founded her reputation on her impeccable melding of colour and print, her garments are every bit as much integral to her vision. She also focuses on the silhouette and the fabrication of each creation and uses "precision engineering to flatter the female form". Printed textiles can be a powerful, illusory tool in reshaping the female form, and Katrantzou is better than most at wielding them to that effect.

RIGHT AND OPPOSITE Embellished velvet dress, Mary Katrantzou, Autumn/Winter 2011–12: A connoisseur's collection of fabulous *objets* was the inspiration for Katrantzou's vision. Fabergé eggs and cloisonné enamel were combined with the exaggerated haute couture shapes of mid-century Paris to create remarkable prints decorated with couture-style embroidery. Katrantzou specifically uses embellishment as a shape and colour enlightener for the digital print.

OPPOSITE *Pencil Dress*, Mary Katrantzou, Autumn/Winter 2012–13: Trompe-l'oeil is a speciality of Katrantzou but here an eddy of real HB pencils is embroidered onto a skirt by Maison Lesage, the Paris haute couture embroidery specialists.

ABOVE Autumn/Winter 2012–13: Katrantzou uses her silhouettes to emphasize her prints and embellishments. Here, a sporty watch appears to cinch an hourglass jacket and skirt combination.

LEFT Layered organza printed dress, Mary Katrantzou, Autumn/Winter 2013–14: Having consolidated her reputation as a master of colour, Katrantzou turned to the black and white landscape photography of Edward Steichen, Clarence White and Alfred Stieglitz to focus attention on other elements of her design.

RIGHT AND
ABOVE Print dress, Mary
Katrantzou, Spring/Summer 2010:
Here, artisanal blown glass was a
starting point for Katrantzou's liquid
effects. The theme was followed
through a fluid trompe-l'oeil frill
curving along the side of the body.
To complement the concept,
Katrantzou commissioned British art
glass artist, Peter Layton, to make
neckpieces and cuffs.

OVERLEAF (left)
Lampshade skirts, Mary Katrantzou,
Autumn/Winter 2011–12. (right)
Lampshade skirts, Mary Katrantzou,
Spring/Summer 2011.
Katrantzou's background as the
daughter of an interior designer and
as a graduate of interior architecture
emerges constantly with references
both oblique and obvious. Her iconic
Lampshade skirts are loaded with a
combination of interior and exterior
details that are ultimately surreal yet
entirely harmonious.

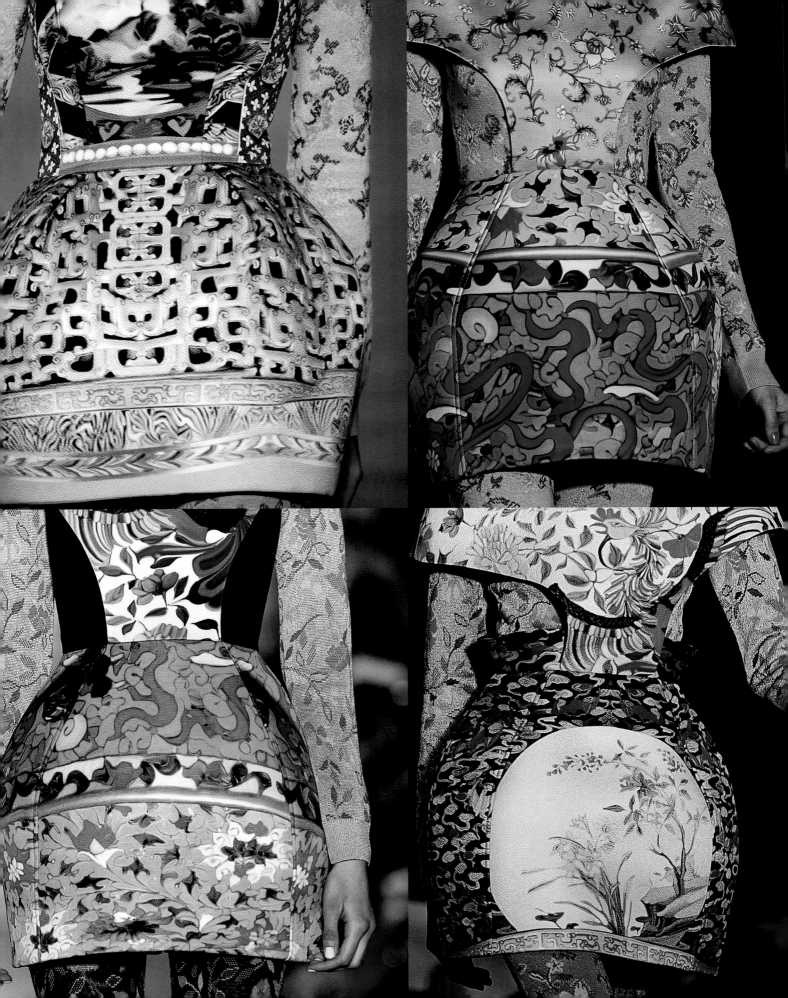

ABOVE AND OPPOSITE *Strip Valley* prints, Mary
Katrantzou, Spring/Summer 2012: Katrantzou builds her prints "pixel by pixel".
She selects pictures that match her vision and pieces them together to make
a silhouette. She then forms the silhouette and the print in Photoshop before
using a mannequin. Here, vibrant stripes are worked across a variety of garments,
each individually formed.

Helmut Lang

The Helmut Lang creative signature is one of the most enduring in the fashion business. Although Lang himself left in 2004 to pursue a career as an artist, his eponymous label retains its main purpose: elegant minimalism. He was succeeded in 2006 by the husband-and-wife team Michael and Nicole Colovos. They have developed their own strong and progressive style, one that references their New York base.

The Helmut Lang label is known for its minimal approach, perfected through the late 1980s and '90s. Reflective, technical fabrics used for tailoring, thermal leathers, slit-and-slash sleeves, asymmetric hems and raw, dark denim were a few of the experimental fashion ideas which Lang moved into the mainstream. The Colovos' update is respectfully different yet true to that test-tube attitude. The same techniques, along with solid and sheer fabric combinations and architectural lines drawn across the body in leather and print, are used in new ways. Their edgy, refined tailoring also reflects those urban lines with their print work.

The singular nature of Helmut Lang calls for a subtle approach to the pattern. There are no shouty graphics or bold messages; instead the prints, like the clothes themselves, are reductive. Graphite strokes, tree bark or pastel smudges are used sparingly and always segue into the collections in alignment with Helmut Lang's customary simplicity. These prints are often the result of experiments with industrial materials and surfaces. The label's use of digital printing is a natural fit for an aesthetic that constantly re-examines the city around it.

For Spring/Summer 2013, the partnership worked with the UK-born, Brooklyn-based tattooist Thomas Hooper to create a series of mandala medallions and florals. Used for boxy jackets, short suits and dresses, they were inspired by the delicate and fantastical illustrations of the nineteenth-century German biologist Ernst Haeckel. Rather than simply scanning the original artwork, Hooper hand-drew the designs, giving them a quality that facsimile prints often lack. Rendered in jacquard or woven, in print as well as applied to materials, they possess the same delicacy as his extravagant tattoos. His work is returned to the body in a new medium.

LEFT Sheer asymmetric dress, Helmut Lang, Spring/Summer 2012: For their prints, the designers often use the work of a contemporary artist as a springboard. Here the lithographs of Richard Serra provide the inspiration for a graphite and yellow brushstroke design.

OPPOSITE *Mandala Wet Print* dress, Helmut Lang, Spring/Summer 2013: A collaborative print, created with tattoo artist Thomas Hooper, is used for a mini-dress with asymmetric glare film underlay.

OPPOSITE LEFT
Asymmetric dress and leggings,
Helmut Lang, Autumn/Winter
2012–13.

OPPOSITE RIGHT
Leather jacket, skirt and leggings,
Helmut Lang, Autumn/Winter
2012–13.

RIGHT Top, skirt, belt and
leggings, Helmut Lang, Autumn/
Winter 2012--3.

OVERLEAF LEFT
Cicadae print, Helmut Lang, Pre-
Autumn 2012: "This print was inspired
by chemically induced spiders and the
webs they created while intoxicated.
We took the complexity of insect
symmetry to create a mirrored layout
on the body. Printing on a very sheer
fine chiffon the textured artwork was
hand painted and then computer-
generated to create the symmetry."
Nicole Colovos

OVERLEAF RIGHT
Pheasant print, Helmut Lang, Resort
2012: "Inspired by Kate MccGwire's
beautiful feather sculptures, we wanted
to capture the wonderful sense of
movement that her sculptures have.
This print was achieved by digitally
altering real feathers, scanning, altering
and recolouring them." *Nicole Colovos*

OPPOSITE *Flesh* print coat dress, Helmut Lang, Autumn/Winter 2013–14: "Richard Prince's Picasso-inspired painterly nudes led us to explore a large-scale engineered layout, creating a textural range by using the shine of the compact duchess satin and overlaying it with a black printed rubber pigment. This print was recreated on multiple fabrics, including leather, with a custom high gloss finish." *Nicole Colovos*

RIGHT Trouser suit, Helmut Lang, Autumn/Winter 2013–14: Richard Prince's Prince/Picasso show also inspired a graphic motif in black and white repeated across the designer's signature sharply tailored trouser suit.

Alexander McQueen

To date, one of the most influential collections in the digital textiles age was to be Lee Alexander McQueen's last full show. *Plato's Atlantis*, created for Spring/Summer 2010, was an exploration of technology's effect upon the natural environment. The title refers to the lost kingdom of Atlantis, the earliest mention of which came from the ancient Greek philosopher Plato, who wrote of a powerful civilization that was sunk by an earthquake. Its fin-de-siècle theme, "...when the waters rise, humanity will go back to the place from whence it came", was examined through McQueen's powerful yet ethereal prints, digitized reworkings of natural patterns and forms. Snakeskin, butterfly wings and jellyfish were morphed into engineered prints, each one unique and created for a single garment.

Plato's Atlantis was to have been one of the first shows to be streamed live on the internet, hosted by the fashion and art website, SHOWstudio.com, although the website crashed in anticipation. The collection, its message and the event itself placed both technology and history at the heart of McQueen's storytelling, as it often did, to create a wildly imaginative vision. "At times like this we need fantasy, not reality. We have enough reality today," explained McQueen to the site's founder, Nick Knight.

Lee Alexander McQueen was born in London in 1969, his route to the catwalk differing from most others. He had already worked as an apprentice tailor on Savile Row, at a theatrical costume house and in the design studios of Koji Tatsuno and Romeo Gigli, two designers known for spectacular textiles, before taking his place at Central Saint Martins in 1991 to complete a Masters degree.

His approach to his work was equally original. A highly inventive and experimental designer, he was also brave in his chosen themes. McQueen's debut collection, *Highland Rape*, for Autumn/Winter 1995–6 commemorated the English slaughter of his Scottish ancestors and featured his "bumster" trousers, cut low enough to reveal buttock cleavage. Controversial first and last, McQueen's creativity nevertheless placed him at the zenith of fashion, along with the tools to create garments and shows worthy of his position.

Throughout McQueen's career, from his MA collection, *Jack the Ripper Stalks his Victims*, to his final, unfinished collection of 16 outfits shown in a gilded Parisian salon soon after his death in February 2010, print was an important part of his narrative. That last display of work included hand-loomed jacquards created from digital photographs of medieval angels and demons. McQueen's successor Sarah Burton, who oversaw the collection's presentation in his place, worked with the designer for 14 years before taking on his mantle. As a former print fashion student, she has maintained the label's reputation for remarkable and innovative textiles.

OPPOSITE *Plato's Atlantis* dress, Alexander McQueen, Spring/Summer 2010: Arguably one of the finest series of digital textile prints, the engineered designs created for each outfit used layers of imagery special to each garment, here embellished with crystals.

LEFT *Plato's Atlantis* dress, Alexander McQueen, Spring/Summer 2010: McQueen's futuristic couture construction provided a deceptively simple canvas for his prints. The necessary shapes were achieved with a highly complex network of seams working in synergy with the prints themselves.

ABOVE *Plato's Atlantis* dress, Alexander McQueen, Spring/Summer 2010: McQueen's visions were all-encompassing. His alien-like theatre of ideas was further augmented with radical 30-cm (12-inch) "armadillo" boots and hair protuberances.

ABOVE RIGHT *Flame* jacket and shirt, Alexander McQueen, Spring/Summer 2012: Semi-engineered print and silk woven artwork by Gary James McQueen with photos of flames manipulated in Photoshop to create shaping up the figure.

OPPOSITE Chiffon and tulle gown, Alexander McQueen, Spring/Summer 2012: Sarah Burton infused her collection with delicate aquatic imagery. Here, chiffon mirrors surf rolling on to the shore.

OPPOSITE Backstage,
Alexander McQueen, Spring/Summer
2009: Natural or man-made? The
crystalline forms that sparkle and burst
across the three dresses featured
in a collection that examined the
industrialization of the natural world.

RIGHT *Plato's Atlantis* dress,
Alexander McQueen, Spring/Summer
2010: Close up and removed from the
catwalk, McQueen's gown reveals its
treasures: shredded chiffon waves at
the hip and an intense hybrid-reptilian
print highlighted with beading.

Erdem Moralioglu

Raised in Canada by an English mother and a Turkish father, and now working in London, Erdem Moralioglu's creative heritage could be the definition of fashion diaspora. The floral connections between Turkey and England are also married in his signature prints. Erdem's flowers are digitally enhanced and reworked to create contemporary versions of an established motif; as much as Moralioglu has focused on this most traditional theme, his outcomes are often far from classic.

Moralioglu studied in Toronto before securing an MA at the Royal College of Art in London. During that period he spent time in the galleries of the Victoria and Albert Museum, a creative laboratory for fashion students. The historical influences on Erdem collections are present throughout but always viewed through the technological prism. It's an aspect of Moralioglu's work that enables him to create elegant yet rigorously modern garments. Every piece, he feels, should have its own individual presence.

"Colour, optimism and oddities" is how Moralioglu characterizes his design signature, and the creative twists that snake through his collections always surprise. Chintzy wallpaper roses are applied to leather, lace appliqué comes in neon pink, and Amish quilt patterns are turned into rich silk coats. He delights in setting up juxtapositions: old and new, bright and subdued, subversive and grown-up. One such combination, black rubber and ladylike lace, was used for his Autumn/Winter 2012–13 collection. Inspired by the strong, artistic personalities of Peggy Guggenheim and Diana Vreeland, he focused on "contradiction" and a colour palette of bright and muted shades brought together in contemporary, reworked florals.

Moralioglu regards each collection as a chapter in his design story and as a reaction to the work that has gone before. He generally designs his collections from the fabrics upwards, his early research including weave, pattern and texture. It's an approach that gives textiles a central role within Erdem collections. While Moralioglu has always worked on his prints digitally, he prefers to do so by trial and error rather than as a clinical and technical exercise. Hand-rendered details such as paint and collage give his prints a human, more naturalistic quality, and Erdem its romantic edge in this mechanized age.

LEFT Top and velvet skirt, Erdem, Autumn/Winter 2011–12: Intense watercolour hues bleed across Moralioglu's polo-neck top. Silk velvet transforms a print with its opulent, iridescent surface.

OPPOSITE Backstage, Erdem, Autumn/Winter 2008–9: Moralioglu has described this print as being a landscape seen from a speeding train. Rich satins from a traditional Italian mill are printed with a design that originated as an image of a crow with rotting fruit. Polished and luxurious, material and print are perfectly matched.

ABOVE Printed cotton gloves and dress, Erdem, Spring/Summer 2012: Fresh, feminine and proper, the mood for this Erdem outfit decorated with a floral and hummingbird print extended to the tips of the model's fingers.

OPPOSITE Floral and lace dress, Erdem, Spring/Summer 2011: Sergei Diaghilev, founder of the Ballets Russes, inspired Moralioglu's collection. Flowers are scattered across a dress with a chiffon bodice, appliquéd and printed with lace highlights.

OVERLEAF (clockwise from left) Spring/Summer 2011: Autumn/Winter 2013–14: Spring/Summer 2011; Autumn/Winter 2011–12. Contemporary floral themes recur throughout Moralioglu's work. Their popularity has been secured by his colour expertise and his injection of unusual, sometimes challenging, hues.

ABOVE Silk shirt, Erdem, Autumn/Winter 2012–13: A silk shirt is given one of Moralioglu's kinetic floral prints and finished with hand-covered silk buttons.

OPPOSITE Cotton appliquéd dress, Erdem, Autumn/Winter 2012–13: A dress is constructed with a patchwork of royal blue sateen, signature prints and appliqués. Dramatic and structured, it is nevertheless intensely feminine and reminiscent of 1950s haute couture.

Peter Pilotto

Japanese "light trucks" – spectacular vehicles scattered with thousands of lights and murals – and illuminated manuscripts from London's British Library may come from different ends of the creative spectrum, but both have inspired Peter Pilotto prints. Pilotto himself is in fact one half of a partnership with Christopher De Vos. Together they have been at the vanguard of the digital print story.

Pilotto, half Austrian, half Italian, and De Vos, half Belgian, half Peruvian, bring together many influences to create their richly vivid and graphic collections. The pair met while studying at Antwerp's Royal Academy of Fine Arts in 2000 and settled in London's East End to forge their careers. While their handwriting is clear, they try to steer away from a formulaic approach. A recent collaboration with the creative director and digital designer Jonny Lu has introduced software, Print Generator, that the designers have called a "digital kaleidoscope". It enables them to generate multitudinous varieties of prints and options.

It's a necessary evolution. Every design used by Peter Pilotto is engineered for the individual garments it decorates, and each garment is designed as a singular piece rather than as a variation on a theme. Sophisticated print placements are the designers' signature, an approach that lends a sense of luxury and individuality to their garments. Their prints deliver colour and energy to the clothes which balance the hyperactive decoration with restrained shapes. The international clientele that favours their work inhabits a world away from the back streets of London's Dalston, where the Peter Pilotto studio is located. But it's the edgy excitement generated there and married with polished, wearable shapes that makes them successful.

Every season, the Peter Pilotto catwalk is infused with the essence of their travels and experiences. For them each collection is like a diary, a reflection of their previous six months. Spring/Summer 2013, for example, began with an inspirational trip to India, the beading for which was also created there. Characteristically, the partnership avoided the region's decorative clichés to free themselves from an obvious conclusion. While Pilotto wanted to make reference to the traditional antique circle mirrors of Indian textiles, he felt a more geometric shape was better suited to his label, so the detail enters the Pilotto prism and emerges as an individual feature. More than a tweak, the digital process is used to heighten the creative process and in doing so produces entirely unique designs.

OPPOSITE *Mars* printed column dress, Peter Pilotto, Autumn/Winter 2011–12: A wool blend dress is softly structured for winter. The print blends and fades to conjure a three-dimensional impression to flatter the loose style.

RIGHT *Dillon Truck* print column dress, Peter Pilotto, Autumn/Winter 2012–13: A curvaceous jersey dress is emblazoned with a Japanese truck-inspired print centre front to balance and toughen its feminine shape.

LEFT Backstage, Peter Pilotto, Autumn/ Winter 2012–13: Bold floral motifs highlighted with blowsy carnations build to form large-scale prints across a variety of outfits and fabrics for a section of the winter collection.

LEFT, OPPOSITE
LEFT AND
OPPOSITE RIGHT

Peter Pilotto, Spring/Summer 2012:
Sporty streamlining through black
delineation and wetsuit zips suggest
a scuba-diving tour of the tropics.
The collection's exotic florals and hot
colours complete the story but not in
an obvious way. Christopher De Vos
and Pilotto use their prints to subvert
clichéd themes and create a fresh
vision of well-trodden ground. The
sweeping cross (far right), created with
print and cutting, is a key, recognizable
signature for the designers.

Prada

Prada's presence as a luxury brand may already have lasted an entire century – Mario Prada opened his doors in Milan's elegant Galleria Vittorio Emanuele II shopping arcade in 1913 – but it is one of fashion's most forward-thinking design houses. For all the company's history, Mario's granddaughter Miuccia Prada, who alongside her husband, Patrizio Bertelli, runs the business, is a relentless modernist. Her avant-garde style and the company's deep-rooted understanding of luxury product is the ideal cocktail for today's fashion industry.

Prada was one of the first luxury labels to widely include digital techniques in 1998. In Autumn/Winter 2004–5, as digital printing was largely being explored by the younger design houses, Prada was blending the work of the nineteenth-century German Romantic landscape painter, Caspar David Friedrich, with Pac Man references to create her cyber aesthetic, "a romanticism between past and future".

Miuccia Prada's ability to deconstruct fashion and present it as an entirely new proposition makes digital printing a natural technique for her to employ. The implied nostalgia used alongside the sharp edges of technology used for the 2004 collection is a recurring theme for Prada although she more often challenges her catwalk viewers by denying them that comfort. Instead she defies the conventions of modern aesthetics, at times choosing "ugly" fabrics or colours above obviously beautiful ones.

For Spring/Summer 2008, Prada printed outfits with illusory, folkloric characters created for her by the Taiwanese-American illustrator James Jean. *Trembled Blossoms* – taken from John Keats' "Ode to Psyche" – emerged from a wallpaper design he created for the label and was expanded to become a promotional film, printed fabrics and a concept for Prada show spaces. The hand-drawn fluidity of the pixie characters and their surreal woodland milieu were ideal for sweeping across and down the body as engineered prints.

For Spring/Summer 2010, Prada again placed digital print at the heart of her season, this time to evoke a positive mood as opposed to brooding charm. Photo prints of a man-made Japanese beach resort were applied to luxurious silk duchesse satin, intended as a dose of optimism against a backdrop of financial crises and political uncertainty. Palm trees, beach umbrellas and lounging holidaymakers were manipulated into fantasy holiday vignettes for a series of jackets, shorts and minidresses. Real yet surreal, they were the perfect expression of contemporary digital textiles.

RIGHT Silk beach prints, Prada, Spring/Summer 2010: The shimmering backgrounds give these photo prints an effervescence that brings them to life. Prada uses intense overlays of colour and unfinished edges to ensure that their picture perfection doesn't become sterile and obvious.

Proenza Schouler

Proenza Schouler is the New York-based partnership of Jack McCollough and Lazaro Hernandez. The pair met at New York's Parson's School of Design where their shared vision was recognised and they were given special permission to create a joint thesis collection. They founded their label, named after the designers' mothers' maiden names, in 2002. Proenza Schouler focuses on womenswear and accessories and has become known for contemporary yet feminine clothes. Their "easy doesn't have to mean sloppy" approach melds sportswear with grown-up tailoring.

The partnership uses digital print for energy and to create a sense of random inspiration – like a Tumblr or a Google search. It also features imagery broken up by solid lines to create a patchwork across the figure. By fragmenting the prints and mixing them with contrasting colours and textures, Proenza Schouler outfits appear as a collection of sampled thoughts. It's a refined fashion response to the snappy, New York milieu of persistent change and noise.

For Autumn/Winter 2011–12 McCollough and Hernandez digitally processed the patterns from traditional Cherokee blankets and had them woven as pixilated woolen jacquard fabrics. For Pre-Autumn 2012, they extracted an aerial view of mountain ranges from Google Earth and based a silk jacquard on its crevices and peaks. This separation from the original is an example of the way digital processes have added a new layer to creativity. Rather than simply reproducing a pattern, the designers influence its future.

The element of subversion is one of the most exciting and challenging aspects of digital printing. Designers can amplify its effect to the point it overwhelms but Proenza Schouler has a more subtle strategy. Like their clothes, McCollough and Hernandez aren't interested in rebellious statements. Maintaining a youthful yet serious fashion business requires an approach that introduces new ideas in a strong, original and wearable way. It also requires them to look beyond the horizon.

McCollough and Hernandez embrace digital culture across their business. Known for their short, sometimes surreal, promotional fashion films, the pair created a Second Life scenario for Spring/Summer 2013. *Desert Tide* features avatar models dancing in a virtual landscape. Whether or not it's a glimpse into our fashion future is debatable but Proenza Schouler's strength is knowing which direction to look in.

LEFT Printed shift dress, Proenza Schouler, Spring/Summer 2011: A print is engineered to shape and highlight a light summer dress. The layered design of neon green foliage and black shadows creates a stormy drama across the plain silk twill body beneath.

OPPOSITE Teal and lime jacket, skirt and bag, Proenza Schouler, Spring/Summer 2013: An intricate patchwork of perforated leather, printed satin and bonded jersey comes together in a unique outfit in a show that blended "technology with craft". For the jacket, designers Jack McCollough and Lazaro Hernandez created a bouclé fabric inspired by Gerhard Richter's teal and black painting "Abstraktes Bild, See", from 1997.

LEFT AND
OPPOSITE Printed silk
dresses, Proenza Schouler, Spring/
Summer 2013: Inspired by the
microblogging platform Tumblr,
the designers used apparently
random images to create vibrant
prints. Grommets and neon studs
were added for texture and to add
a weighted swing to the garments.

Masha Reva

Masha Reva is a young designer whose career has emerged alongside digital printing, a technique she uses throughout her work. Born in Odessa, Ukraine, she comes from a family of artists: her father is a sculptor/architect and her mother a former fashion student at Saint Petersburg's Muhina Academy of Arts. On a visit to London in 2004, aged 17, Reva filled a sketchbook with drawings of the people she saw on the streets in the Camden area. Inspired by them, she decided at that point to become a fashion designer.

Reva's use of digital print is directly linked to her habit of relentless sketching. "I adore drawing and I'm used to translating my feelings with the help of anything that I can draw," she explains. "This is my nature: I love to make sketches, and I feel that digital print is a symbiosis of both clothes and drawings – my two main obsessions."

In bringing the two together, Reva starts the design process with those sketches. "Firstly, I try to imagine a mood of what I want to create," she says. "I think print and shape should be developed at the same time as it should be all balanced, although usually the print is more important for me. I am a visual person and my inspiration always comes from strong imagery."

Because fashion is an end product, the textiles that create it have always been an act of collaboration. The new breed of designers who, with digital design, are able to combine fabric and construction within their work are finding new ways to form creative partnerships. Reva has worked on several collaborative photography projects to showcase her prints, powerful images which serve as an extension of her work. "The team is very important to me when it comes to creating a visual communication with an audience," she says. "Without their help, my ideas would not be shown from all the perspectives they are today."

For Reva, digital printing reflects her magpie character and our modern state of constant sensory overload: "It's all about our contemporary reality – today we have too much information. I think digital print reflects this clash of many available sources of inspiration. It's exciting to collect visual inspiration – I can recycle it to become something that will form a whole new concept."

LEFT, OPPOSITE AND OVERLEAF
Merging, Masha Reva, 2012: "Today a human is surrounded by a huge amount of information while social networks and blogs bring us an opportunity to create a superficial representation of ourselves in the Web... Becoming a part of virtual reality, a computer data, we merge within the boundless informational field that is the internet... [It] has a certain connection with print... The principles laid within are over-information, adaptation and merging in the mass of images today." *Masha Reeva*

"*Becoming a part of virtual reality, a computer data, we merge within the boundless informational field that is the Internet. The situation within the visual stream we deal with every day — from one point it is related to the layering of information within our mind, from the other, it has a certain connection with print.*" Masha Reva

ABOVE Sketches for Graduation collection, Masha Reva, Autumn/Winter 2010–11: Reva approaches her fashion and print design as a single process: "I think print and shape should be developed at the same time as it should be all balanced." *Masha Reva*

BELOW Print designs for Graduation collection, Masha Reva, Autumn/Winter 2010–11: "Firstly, I try to imagine a mood of what I want to create. Then I work on prints in parallel with creating a collection." *Masha Reva*

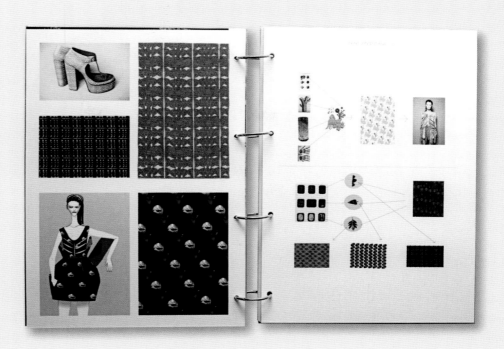

RIGHT Sketchbooks for Graduation collection, Masha Reva, Autumn/Winter 2010–11.

OVERLEAF *Botanical Layers*, Masha Reva and Syndicate of Kiev, 2012: Reva and the young Ukrainian brand, Syndicate, explore their yearning for the natural environment and their overloaded informational landscape through original prints applied to sweatshirts.

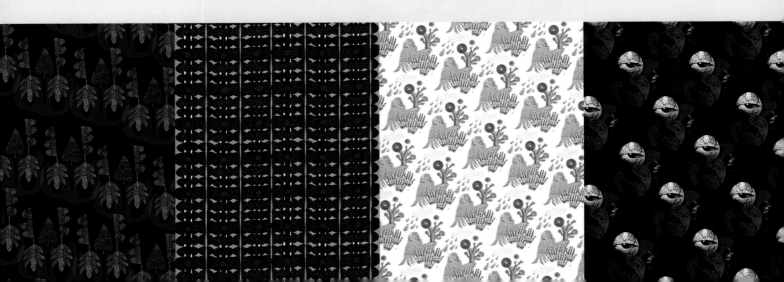

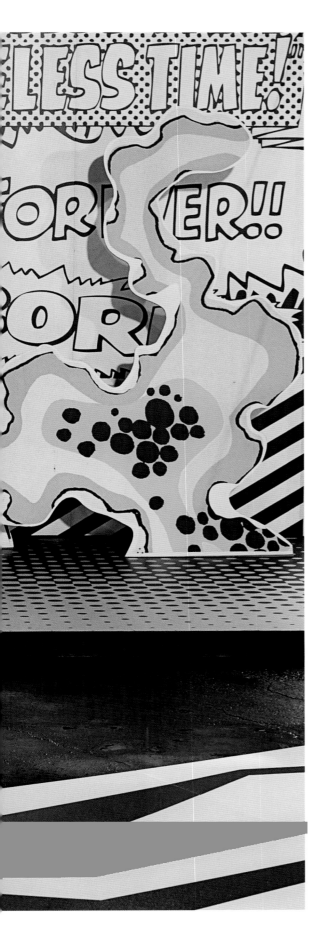

Romance Was Born

Romance Was Born is the Sydney-based partnership of fashion designers Anna Plunkett and Luke Sales. The pair met during their studies at East Sydney Technical College and their coming together was a simple meeting of minds and ideas. Their label was created in 2005 and has become known for its spectacular and chimerical prints. These designs form the basis of their collections, evoking and explaining the ideas behind them. Both Sales and Plunkett share an obsession for detail and craft, with embellishment featuring throughout their collections. This sumptuous aesthetic blends print with appliqué, tie-dye and crochet. One dress, worn by the actress Cate Blanchett, was crocheted by Sales' mother, an example of the handcrafting that humanizes their collections.

Romance Was Born's inspirations are just as eclectic. One season they explore Marvel comic characters, the next they dip into Frances Hodgson Burnett's classic Victorian children's book, *Little Lord Fauntleroy*. Explaining a complicated narrative is a challenge for a designer. Romance Was Born chooses to communicate them most often through print, which has been a mainstay of their work since their first collection.

Plunkett and Sales have seen print processes develop during that time. "We have worked a lot on hand-printed textile development in the past; things like devoré prints, textural puff paint, discharge printing and over-dyeing," says Plunkett. "When we first started working together in 2005 we began to experiment with digital printing. At the time it wasn't very common, and very expensive, but nowadays that's not the case and it's a major technique for us."

The team repeatedly works with Australian artists. Del Kathryn Barton, Patrick Dougherty and Esme Timbery, a noted indigenous Australian artist who works mainly with shells, have all created original work for Romance Was Born. The process of getting the prints on to the catwalk is also a collaborative one. "We have worked with a few graphic designers very closely over the last seven years," explains Plunkett. "Each season it's a different working style, but usually they work from our studios. We brief them and then we go back and forth with conceptualizing until we arrive at the result we're looking for." Illusory and uncompromising, the results are always original.

LEFT AND OVERLEAF *Berserkergang* collection, Romance Was Born, Spring/Summer 2012: "We really wanted to break down the elements of the comic look, rather than focusing on the more obvious things. [American comic book artist] Jack Kirby played such an important part in the comic book world as one of the true originators of popular comics. *Berserkergang* is a mash-up of Kirby-inspired optical dots, but also other classic Marvel characters that were abstracted and played with to carry through the narrative of the collection." *Anna Plunkett*

PAGES 182—3 The *Oracle* collection, Spring/Summer 2011.

PAGES 184—5 *Lil Lord Fauntleroy* collection, Spring/Summer 2013.

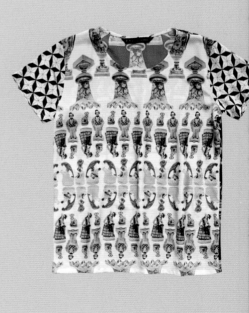

LEFT *She Hulk* shorts, Romance Was Born, Spring/Summer 2013: This was shown in Australia as part of the *Berserkergang* collection, in which the designers pieced together comic book art with powerful, contrasting graphics.

OPPOSITE Striped dress, Romance Was Born, Spring/Summer 2013: Stripes create an optical illusion the length of a stretch column dress. Cartoony and dramatic though the engineered print is, the dress is classic and simple.

Jonathan Saunders

Intense ombré graduations and large-scale placement prints are two of the ways Jonathan Saunders uses digital printing in his collections. From season to season he challenges himself to create new ideas, one season deliberately choosing "ugly" fabrics. Colour is his strength and his starting point, however.

Raised in Glasgow by his Jehovah's Witness parents, Saunders' early life was a modest and spartan affair. Having put himself through college and after first studying furniture design, he gained a BA in Printed Textiles from the Glasgow School of Art followed by an MA from Central Saint Martins in London. Saunders quickly earned his reputation for creating vivid labour-intensive prints. Soon after graduation, Alexander McQueen sought out Saunders to design a print for him – the iconic bird-of-paradise that featured in McQueen's Spring/Summer 2003 collection – and other design houses quickly followed.

But that wasn't to be his trajectory: Saunders decided to begin his own collection in 2003, and went on to become one of the most successful examples of a textiles designer turned fashion designer. It is a facet of Saunders' work that sets him apart from his contemporaries. Once the digital revolution revealed itself and presented him with fresh avenues to follow, he was certainly in the best position to project his textiles background.

Saunders regards his trademark piece as a "colourful A-line shift dress". It's a formula that has worked for women since the American designer Lilly Pulitzer created it in the 1950s as a beach dress. The simplicity of its shape and purpose makes it an ideal backdrop for prints and creates a hallmark piece that women can return to each season. Equally, Saunders' background as a print designer enables him to succeed in the enduring sphere of the printed scarf. It's a piece that can be an important dimension of a designer's business, but can also extend their reach if they're able to create signature prints, which Saunders has done with his ubiquitous *Ombré Spot* print.

The commercial aspect of his clothes and accessories is very much a focus. He is one of a new generation of designers for whom a professional approach to business is second nature. It's what enables Jonathan Saunders to maintain and develop his contribution to modern textiles.

LEFT Print dress, Jonathan Saunders, Spring/Summer 2005: Saunders marked himself out from the start as a superb colourist. Here, he skillfully combines a multitude of hues within a Bauhaus-inspired engineered print.

OPPOSITE Collection finale, Jonathan Saunders, Spring/Summer 2005: A complete collection can be best appreciated when the outfits appear together at the end of a show. As a display of work by one of the most successful print designers, Saunders' vision retains its impact and freshness today.

LEFT Shirt and skirt, Jonathan
Saunders, Autumn/Winter 2011–12:
Saunders referenced the saturated
colourwork of the American artist and
photographer Paul Outerbridge for his
collection. Great expertise is needed to
bring together shades and tones that
are not natural partners in this way.

OPPOSITE Backstage,
Jonathan Saunders, Autumn/
Winter 2010–11: Variations on dots,
fades and blocks create graphic
combinations across three outfits.

OVERLEAF Menswear
collection, Jonathan Saunders, Spring/
Summer 2013: Saunders' rainbow
ombré spots have become a signature
look for the designer. They have been
used across a wide variety of fabrics
and colourways in both the menswear
and womenswear collections.

Topshop Unique

Launched in 2001, Unique is the designer offshoot of Topshop, the UK's leading high-street fashion company. Topshop Unique was the first fast fashion brand to appear at London Fashion Week, in 2005, and has, although unwittingly, democratized designer fashion. Seeing creative clothes shown on an international catwalk stage and sold in a high-street store has stretched the expectations of customers. Innovative fabrics and techniques that would previously have stayed at the top of the market have become commonplace throughout the chain. Digital printing is one such advancement.

The Unique design team uses digital printing to expand its creative reach. Emma Farrow, head of design for Topshop, says, "Depending on the season and inspiration for the collection, sometimes we find that the more traditional printing methods can limit our creativity. Digital printing offers limitless colour possibilities, super scales and effects that elevate our print to exciting levels." Topshop maintains an in-house print team that works on both Topshop main collections and Unique. They use a variety of printing techniques, from hand painting to digital printing, depending on the season and specific trend requirements.

The combination of mass-market availability and a designer approach makes the Unique shows popular events. In September 2012, more than two million people from 100 countries watched the online video of the Spring/Summer 2013 catwalk collection after it was live-streamed. Topshop also offered customers the chance to shop for clothes and accessories as they emerged on the catwalk, with one dress selling out while it was still being shown.

Pushing new digital technologies is at the heart of Topshop's strategy, both in terms of design and commerce. In February 2013, it scored another first by introducing Model Cam, a sports channel-inspired interface that allowed viewers to switch from a camera focused on the catwalk to a micro camera worn by models including Cara Delevingne and Jourdan Dunn. Viewers could access a specially created "Be The Buyer" app to select and share their favourite catwalk looks. It also happened to be an invaluable resource for the company's buying team, instantly identifying the most popular pieces.

Unique has paved the way for other collections rooted in the high street to cross over into designer territory at the catwalk level. It continues to innovate away from the catwalk, too.

OPPOSITE *Baroque Luxe* print, Topshop Unique, Christmas 2012: "Digitized photographic references of jewels and pearls were combined with Italian ceiling frescoes – a great source of inspiration for one of our Christmas trends last year." *Emma Farrow*

ABOVE RIGHT *Baroque Luxe* dress, Topshop Unique, Christmas 2012: The print is engineered across a slender sheath dress with outsize pearls focused at the neckline.

OVERLEAF Multicolour silk dress (left) and multicolour silk shirt (right), Topshop Unique, Autumn/Winter 2013–14: "Heritage carpets and wallpapers were recreated and digitized... The blurring of lines and pixelated effect was important for us, as was play with large and small scales." *Emma Farrow*

PAGES 198–9 *Kaleidoscopic Bohemia* print, Topshop Unique, Spring/Summer 2011: "Here, we used ethereal imagery combining both photographic and illustrative sources together." *Emma Farrow*

Iris van Herpen

Working at the interface between fashion and technology, Iris van Herpen is a unique designer. She fuses traditional techniques with innovative fabrics and processes. These include rapid prototyping – digital 3-D printing – to create sculptural, innovative work. Despite the modernity of her challenging work, van Herpen's collections have won her a place at the heart of French fashion. Since July 2011 when she made her debut with her *Capriole* collection, van Herpen has shown at Paris Haute Couture Week. As a member of the Chambre Syndicale de la Haute Couture, her name sits alongside the greatest couturiers from fashion history, yet her vision appears a futuristic one.

Van Herpen graduated from the ArtEZ Institute of the Arts in Arnhem in the Netherlands in 2006. She completed an internship with Alexander McQueen, where she witnessed his devotion to state-of-the-art techniques and dramatic visualizations. In 2007 she launched her own label; each collection since has contained a powerful narrative from which utilitarian garments rarely emerge.

Crystallization, shown in 2010, explored her fascination for the "secrets and invisibility of water". It was the first to feature 3-D-printed pieces, made in collaboration with the London-based architect Daniel Widrig and printed by the additive manufacturer (3-D printer) .MGX by Materialise. Three-dimensional technologies can produce shapes and products that would otherwise be impossible to create. In van Herpen's case, her pieces are initially planned in Photoshop. She then works with an architect to develop a 3-D model, which is laser-printed onto a polymer over the course of a week. After careful hand-finishing, the dress emerges, an exact copy of her original plan. In 2011, *Time* magazine selected a 3-D dress from van Herpen's *Escapism* collection as one of their 50 Best Inventions of that year.

Technology allows van Herpen to materialize her concepts as garments. A dress that "cocoons the body as would a bath of warm water" becomes possible in a way like never before. Parts of her earlier collections seem as if they were prototypes awaiting the tools to create the final product.

Collaboration is central to Iris van Herpen's success, as it is for any couturier who relies on an army of specialists. Van Herpen, however, creates within the realm of scientists and architects. It's they who construct her work rather than pattern cutters and seamstresses. Is she envisioning the future of fashion with her digital pieces? "I'm super-curious about everything that's not quite possible yet," says van Herpen. "Couture is the laboratory."

OPPOSITE Finale, *Hybrid Holism* collection, Iris van Herpen, Haute Couture, Autumn/Winter 2012–13: The project "Hylozoic Ground" by the Canadian architect and artist Philip Beesley inspired van Herpen for this collection. Hylozoism – the ancient belief that all matter is in some sense alive – reveals itself through a series of "organic" garments conjured through a variety of digital and physical processes.

ABOVE *Capriole*, shown at Berlin Fashion Week, Spring/Summer 2012: Van Herpen, who also showed *Capriole* as her debut in Paris during the Haute Couture season, creates external skeletons using 3-D printing created with architect Isaie Bloch and with Sven Hermans at manufacturing company Materialise.

OPPOSITE Jacket and skirt, *Voltage* collection, Iris van Herpen, Haute Couture, Spring/Summer 2013: Van Herpen seeks to describe light and electricity in a collection of garments created through laser cutting and printing alongside traditional haute couture techniques.

Dries Van Noten

Even in a business of individuals, Dries Van Noten stands apart from his contemporaries. Since 1986, the year he launched his eponymous label, he has developed a unique and familiar aesthetic. "I'm known for colour and prints and embroideries," he told *Vogue* in 2007. "Normally the more clashing it is, the more that I like it!"

Van Noten had solid fashion foundations from which to work. Born in Belgium's seaport Antwerp in 1958, he is the third generation in a family of tailors. In the 1970s his father opened a multi-brand boutique where he sold collections such as Ungaro and Ferragamo. With his father, Van Noten visited the catwalk shows in Milan, Düsseldorf and Paris – a valuable insight into the business of fashion.

In 1976, Van Noten enrolled at Antwerp's Royal Academy of Fine Arts, alongside Dirk Bikkembergs, Ann Demeulemeester, Walter van Beirendonck, Marina Yee and Dirk van Saene, In the mid-1980s, they travelled together in a van to show in London, where they were dubbed the "Antwerp Six". By presenting a united vision, their avant-garde and distinct style was magnified. It established their international presence, which for Dries Van Noten meant showing in Paris.

A Dries Van Noten outfit often comprises a multiplicity of prints and layers. Throughout his career he has explored the garments and shapes of Asia, mixing them with the European tailoring of his childhood. This collision of eras, cultures and colours makes digital printing an ideal technique for Van Noten. With it he can mix and meld imagery to create exciting and unique collages. He creates large areas of pattern and colour which, as a designer who favours longer lengths, are showcased perfectly on Van Noten's catwalk.

The variability of his exotic prints, weaves and textures makes Dries Van Noten a designer for men and women who value individual style. His look, though expensive, isn't about visible logos and totem items. Rather, he assumes that his customers have the personality to edit the trends and to dress the way that suits them. For this reason he is a favourite of those who work in the creative industries. Rather than enforcing a rigid concept, he offers variation and contrast through his print and garments.

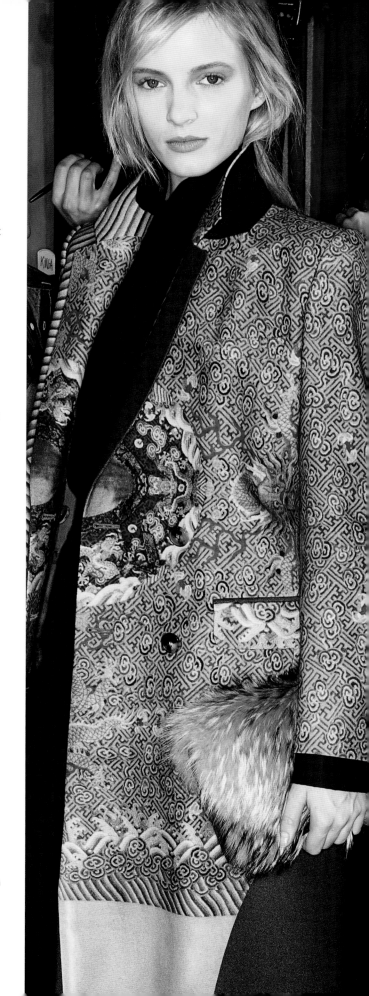

OPPOSITE Backstage, Dries Van Noten, Autumn/Winter 2008–9: Spectacular multi-printed, layered dressing is Van Noten's métier. Here, his silks bear a profusion of colours and manipulated images, both painterly and photographic.

RIGHT Backstage, Dries Van Noten, Autumn/Winter 2012–13: Van Noten photographed costumes and textiles from China, Japan and Korea at the Victoria and Albert Museum to create his prints for this collection. A coat is engineered from a robe design with a central motif and a deep gold border.

ABOVE Backstage, Dries Van Noten, Autumn/Winter 2012–13: Van Noten lines up with his models. His textured wool-silk coats and silk satin dress are formed of abstract oriental print panels.

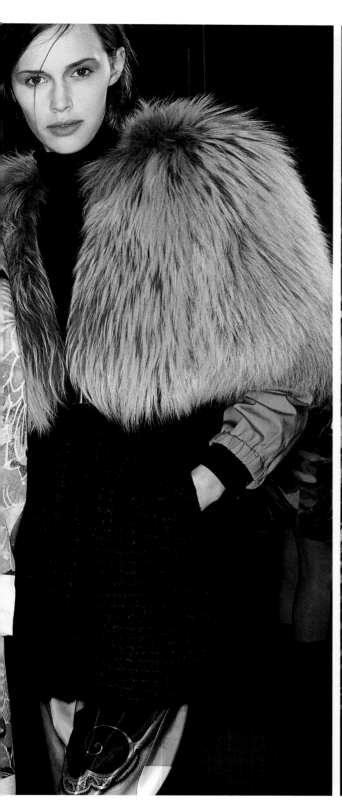

ABOVE Backstage, Dries Van Noten, Autumn/Winter 2011–12:
Sixty-five separate fabrics comprised a collection that referenced David Bowie's
Ziggy Stardust and Russian constructivism. Van Noten's ability to piece
together a disparate variety of themes, colours and materials results in ever-
individual combinations.

LEFT Summer separates, Dries
Van Noten, Autumn/Winter 2008–9:
Digital printing offers the designer
the limitless variety his style requires.
"I worked on printing several different
patterns on one piece of material,"
he told *Vogue*, "so that you can end
up wearing four or five prints in just
a couple of pieces."

OPPOSITE Printed jacket,
Dries Van Noten, Autumn/Winter
2012–13: A soft, wool-blend jacket
is printed with all-over landscape
patterning. The designer frequently
uses antique ethnic textiles in his
eclectic mix of references.

Matthew Williamson

Born in Manchester and trained at Central Saint Martins in London, Matthew Williamson graduated in 1994 with a BA in Fashion Design and Printed Textiles. In 1997, Williamson formed his company with CEO Joseph Velosa, and debuted with his *Electric Angels* collection at London Fashion Week. The collection comprised just 14 bright outfits, but in persuading models Kate Moss and Helena Christensen and his friend Jade Jagger to model for him, Williamson was able to bring his fresh, vivid style to the widest possible audience.

Williamson's design signatures are colour and print, with India's saturated, exotic hues and textiles techniques a major inspiration. They have highlighted and at times drenched his work, making digitally printed textiles an ideal vehicle for him. It enables the designer to create highly detailed patterns coloured with intense palettes.

Married with his Bohemian socialite style, Williamson's outfits have been characterized as party clothes for wealthy, cosmopolitan women. That said, his often subtle and sophisticated digital prints are an interesting variation. Williamson's prints are never aggressive or gauche; they always fit into an easily understood, commercial story. It's a grown-up response and one that contrasts with the abandoned approach to print seen with other designers. He intelligently applied the benefits of digital printing to what he was already doing rather than treating it as a trend to be mined.

For Spring/Summer 2013, Williamson used the work of the New York artist Shane McAdams, who created abstract dreamscapes and patterns that appear to be digitally created although they are made using physical processes for his "Synthetic Landscape" series. Williamson transferred McAdams' skylines and patterns on to simple silk tailoring using digital printing. Together they crafted a look that is urbane and modern.

Williamson's work has also included a three-year stint, from 2005, as the creative director at the Italian house best known for its prints, Emilio Pucci. It was a natural match for a designer whose outfits for smart, social women are the modern-day equivalent of those created by Pucci himself for his aristocratic friends in the 1950s. Williamson's own contribution to this more recent chapter in fashion textiles has been less flamboyant than some. Ever the pragmatist, instead he has created a wearable, relaxed vision for his wearers.

LEFT Evening gown, Matthew Williamson, Autumn/Winter 2012–13: A splintered burst of pattern creates a spectacular design across Williamson's gown. Blooms at the bottom of the print disintegrate toward the shoulder and deeper shards of claret sink to the hem to create a balanced, elongated effect.

OPPOSITE Backstage, Matthew Williamson, Spring/Summer 2009: Sleek, sexy dresses with a monochrome technical edge layered over a soft ombré background. Slicks of bugle beads at the neck and waist add definition and polish to Williamson's prints.

OVERLEAF (left to right) Autumn/Winter 2006–7; Spring/Summer 2012; Spring/Summer 2011; Autumn/Winter 2007–8.

The artist Shane McAdams' "Synthetic Landscape" dreamscapes were digitally rendered onto pieces for Williamson's Spring/Summer 2013 collection, shown on these pages. Here McAdams discusses the ideas behind the collaboration with author Tamasin Doe.

Tamasin Doe: In your artist's statement you say, "I hope to evoke the duality between the actual and the artificial as it is conveyed through idealized representations of order and beauty". Is it too literal to say that your partnership with Matthew Williamson, in which your work is transformed into something essentially artificial and of the moment, does exactly that?

Shane McAdams: I would say that is a more literal interpretation than what I was thinking. However, now that you mention it, that's a very interesting idea. My thought was actually more about the notion that abstractions, formed by processes, are more "real" or "natural" than an illusion of a landscape fashioned from oil paint. But now that the abstraction, originally an actual event, has been digitized and turned into clothing, wouldn't it be great to paint them in oil paint and show the original next to it?

Tamasin Doe: Your methods for achieving your images are physical, yet one of their qualities is a perfection that suggests digital intervention (our "misread"). Did the notion of committing them digitally to fabric feel like a particularly appropriate one when you were approached?

Shane McAdams: It actually didn't. I wasn't completely against it... However, this is where I give Matthew credit, and in the end why I feel a little ashamed with the credit he's so generously given to me for this project – because he so completely transformed my work that it really was about him using it as a medium to make something all his own. And I'm completely comfortable with those terms.

Tamasin Doe: Digitally rendered textile prints seem to be a perfect point at which artists and designers can collaborate. What makes the process interesting from an artist's perspective?

Shane McAdams: For me it's interesting because it's something I know *nothing* about. I'm completely analog as a concept. My work is founded on the idea that a few elegant moves with commonplace materials, harnessing the basic laws of physics, can actually make something better than a hand or a computer can render. The fact that Matthew came to me and not to a computer terminal for source material is confirmation of that.

Designer Directory

Agi & Sam
http://agiandsam.com

Michael Angel
www.michaelangel.net

Antoni & Alison
www.antoniandalison.co.uk

Basso & Brooke
www.bassoandbrooke.com

Hussein Chalayan
http://husseinchalayan.com

Tsumori Chisato
www.tsumorichisato.com

Clover Canyon
www.clovercanyon.com

Giles Deacon
http://giles-deacon.com

Dolce & Gabbana
www.dolcegabbana.com

Fabitoria
http://fabitoria.blogspot.com/

Holly Fulton
www.hollyfulton.com

Josh Goot
www.joshgoot.com

Givenchy
www.givenchy.com

Prabal Gurung
www.prabalgurung.com

Jenny Kao
http://jenkao.com

Mary Katrantzou
www.marykatrantzou.com

Alexander McQueen
www.alexandermcqueen.co.uk

Helmut Lange
www.helmutlang.com

Prada
www.prada.com

Proenza Schouler
www.proenzaschouler.com

Erdem Moralioglu
www.erdem.com

Peter Pilotto
www.peterpilotto.com

Masha Reva
www.mashareva.com

Romance Was Born
http://romancewasborn.com

Jonathan Saunders
www.jonathan-saunders.com

Topshop Unique
www.topshop.com

Iris van Herpen
www.irisvanherpen.com

Dries Van Noten
www.driesvannoten.be

Matthew Williamson
www.matthewwilliamson.com

Index

Page numbers in *italic* refer to illustration captions. Collections are indexed under brands with abbreviations S/S for Spring/Summer and A/W for Autumn/Winter.

A

accessories
    bags *166*
    belts *139*
    gloves *152*
    scarves *40*, 188
Agi & Sam 12, 18–23
    2012–13 (A/W) *18*
    2013 (S/S) *18*, *23*; (A/W) *22*
Alexander McQueen 13, 18, 144–9, 200
    2003 (S/S) 12, 188
    2009 (S/S) *149*
    2010 (S/S) 145, *145*, *146*, *149*
    2012 (S/S) *146*
Angel, Michael 24–33
animatronics 53
Antoni & Alison 15, 34–41
    2004 (S/S) *34*
    2012–13 (A/W) 34, *35*
    2013 (S/S) *35*
Antwerp Six 205
Araki, Nobuyoshi *108*
archival textiles 13
Art Deco 91
ArtEZ Institute of the Arts 200
Australian Fashion Week 103

B

Baroque prints *195*
Barton, Del Kathryn 179
Basi, Armand 18
Basso & Brooke 42–51
    2009 (S/S) 42, *49*
    2010 (S/S) *10*, 42
    2011 (S/S) *49*
    2012 (S/S) *49*
    Dorchester Collection *44*
Basso, Bruno 12, 42
Bath, Marquess of *22*
Bauhaus 91, *188*
beach prints *164*
Beaton, Cecil *70*
Beesley, Philip *200*
Berlin Fashion Week *202*
Bertelli, Patrizio 164
Bertroche, Ryan *24*
Bigwood, Fleet 13

Bikkembergs, Dirk 205
bird-of-paradise prints 12, 98, 188
Blanchett, Cate 179
Blanks, Tim 42
Blass, Bill 15, 108
Bloch, Isaie *202*
Bohemia print *200*
Bowie, David *207*
Brooke, Christopher 12, 42
Bunka Fashion School 58
Burakowski, Antoni 15, 34
Burnett, Frances Hodgson 179
Burton, Sarah 145, *146*

C

Cambridge, Duchess of 108
Cambridge Satchel Company *44*
capes *74*
Cardin, Pierre 126
Castelbajac, Jean-Charles de 70
Central Saint Martins 13, 42, 53, 70, 98, 114, 126, 145, 188, 210
Chalayan, Hussein 12, 52–7
Chang, Fabiana 82
Chisato, Tsumori 58–63, 120
Christensen, Helena 210
Christopher Kane 114–19
    2010 114
    2011 (Resort) 114, *118*; (S/S) *117*
    2013 (S/S) 114, *114*; (A/W) *117*
Chung, Alexa *114*
Cicadae print *139*
Clover Canyon 64–9
    2012–13 (A/W) *64*; (Resort) *69*
    2013 *64*; (Pre-Autumn) *69*; (A/W) *17*
coats *18*, *49*, *206*
Colonial Williamsburg Foundation, Virginia, USA 13
Colovos, Michael 136
Colovos, Nicole 136, *139*
Converse *44*
Cotton, Sam 12, 15, 18

D

De Vos, Christopher 12, 159, *162*
Deacon, Giles 70–5, 114
Delamore, Philip 12
Delevingne, Cara 195

Deller, Jeremy *74*
Demeulemeester, Ann 205
Design Museum 42
Diaghilev, Sergei *152*
digital printing 6, 10
    environmental footprint 15
    software 12, *134*, *146*, 159, 200
Dillon Truck print *159*
Doherty, Patrick 179
Dolce, Domenico 76
Dolce & Gabbana 76–81
    2009 76
    2012–13 (A/W) *76*, *80*
    2013 (A/W) *76*, *80*; (S/S) 76, *76*
dresses 15, *29*, *32*, *49*, *56*, *58*, *60*, *64*, *98*, *103*, *111–12*,
    114, *117*, *126*, *129–31*, *156*, *168*, *186*, *188*, *206*, *210*
    asymmetric *136*, *139*
    coat dress *143*
    cocktail *70*   , *96*
    column *10*, *31*, *53*, *159*
    dungaree *91*, *93*
    gowns *44*, *53*, *146*, *210*
    mini-dress *122*
    Plato's Atlantis dress *145–6*, *149*
    sheath *195*
    shift *166*
    shirt-dress *120*, *125*
    two-in-one *53*
Dries Van Noten 120, 204–9
    2008–9 (A/W) *205*, *208*
    2011–12 (A/W) *207*
    2012–13 (A/W) *205*, *206*, *208*
Dunn, Jourdan 195

E
East Sydney Technical College 179
Edinburgh College of Art 91
Elbaz, Alber 91
embroidery *10*, *126*, *129*
engineered printing 6, 12
Erdem Moralioglu 150–7
    2008–9 (A/W) *150*
    2011 (S/S) *152*; (A/W) *150*, *152*
    2012 (S/S) *152*; (A/W) 150, *152*
    2013–14 (A/W) *152*
Escher, M C *91*

F
Fabitoria 82–9
    2013 (S/S) *85*
Farrow, Emma 13, 195
Farrow, Linda *108*

Fashion Digital Studio 12
Fashion East 91
Fashion Fringe Awards 42
Fellini, Federico 76
Flower Brocade print *104*
Franke, Bette *76*
Friedrich, Caspar David 164
Fulton, Holly 90–7

G
Gabbana, Stefano 76
Galaxy prints *114*, *118*
Gigli, Romeo 145
Giles Deacon 70–5, 114
    2005–6 (A/W) *70*
    2009 (S/S) *70*
    2011–12 (A/W) *70*
    2012 *74*; (S/S) *70*
    2013–14 (A/W) *70*
Givenchy 98–101
    2011–12 (A/W) 98, *98*
    2012 (S/S) 98, *100*
    2013–14 (A/W) 98
Glasgow School of Art 188
Google Earth 166
Goot, Josh 102–7
Graham-Dixon, Andrew 53
Guggenheim, Peggy 150
Gurung, Prabal 108–13

H
Haeckel, Ernst 136
Hartnell, Norman *117*
haute couture 98, *156*, *200*, *202*
Helmut Lang 136–43
    2012 (S/S) *136*; (Pre-Autumn) *139*; (A/W) *139*;
    (Resort) *139*
    2013 (S/S) 136, *136*; (A/W) *143*
Hermans, Sven *202*
Hermès 42
Hernandez, Lazaro 166, *166*
Holly Fulton 90-7
    2011 (S/S) *93*
    2012 (S/S) *93*, *96*; (A/W) *96*
    2013–14 (A/W) *91*
Hooper, Thomas 136, *136*
Hussein Chalayan 12, 52–7
    2009 (S/S) *53*
    2012–13 (A/W) *56*
    2013 (S/S) *53*, *56*; (A/W) *53*
Hylozoism *200*

I

Iris Van Herpen 12, 200–3
   2010 200
   2011 (S/S) *200*
   2012 (S/S) *202*; (A/W) *200*
   2013 (S/S) *202*

J

jackets *4*, *64*, *69*, *91*, *139*, *146*, *166*, *202*, *208*
Jagger, Jade 210
Japan Fashion Week 58
Jean, James 164
Jen Kao 120–5
   2011 (S/S) *120*, *122*
   2012 (S/S) *120*, *125*
Jonathan Saunders 12, 188–93
   2005 (S/S) *188*
   2010–11 (A/W) *190*
   2011–12 (A/W) *190*
   2013 (S/S) *190*
Josh Goot 102–7
   2009 *104*; (S/S) *103*
   2010–11 (A/W) *104*
   2011 (S/S) *103*
   2012 (S/S) *104*
jumpsuits *60*

K

kaftans *29*
kaleidoscope effect 12
Kane, Christopher 114–19
Kane, Tammy 114
Kao, Jen 120–5
Kao, Victoria 82
Katrantzou, Mary 6, *6*, 15, 126–35
Keats, John 164
Kingston University 42
Kirby, Jack *179*
Knight, Nick 145
Koons, Jeff *10*, *42*

L

Lagerfeld, Karl 18
Lang, Helmut 136
Lanvin 91
Layton, Peter *131*
Le Callennec, Eline *10*, 13
LEDs 53
leggings *29*, *122*, *139*
Liberty 15
London 2012 Festival *74*
London College of Fashion 12

London Fashion Week 13, 195, 210
L'Oreal Melbourne Fashion Festival *104*
Lu, Jonny 159

M

Maison Lesage *129*
Manchester School of Art 18
Mandala print *136*
Mars print *159*
Mary Katrantzou 6, 15, 126–35
   2008 126
   2010 (S/S) *131*
   2011 (S/S) *131*; (A/W) 13, 126, *126*, *131*
   2012 (S/S) *10*, *134*; (A/W) *129*
   2013 (S/S) 6; (A/W) 126, *130*
Masha Reva 170–7
   2010–11 (A/W) *174–5*
   2012 *170*
Materialise 200, *202*
Matthew Williamson 210–13, 214
   2006–7 (A/W) *210*
   2007–8 (A/W) *210*
   2009 (S/S) *210*
   2011 (S/S) *210*
   2012 (A/W) *210*; (S/S) *210*
   2013 (S/S) 210
Mawston, Emma 15
McAdams, Shane 210, 214
MccGwire, Kate *139*
McCollough, Jack 166, *166*
McQueen, Alexander 12, 15, 18, 144–9, 188, 200
McQueen, Gary James 12, *146*
Mdumulla, Agape 12, 15, 18
Menkes, Suzy 114
menswear 18–23, *80*, 98, *100*, *146*, *190*, *208*
Michael Angel 24–33
   2008–9 (A/W) *29*, *31*, *32*
   2009–10 (A/W) *33*; (S/S) *24*
   2010 (S/S) *24*, *29*
   2011–12 (A/W) *24*
   2012 (S/S) 24
Miyake, Issey 58
Model Cam 195
Moore, Demi 108
Moralioglu, Erdem 150–7
Moran, Aaron 108, *111*
Moss, Kate 210
Muhina Academy of Arts 170

N

needlepoint prints *18*, *23*, *80*
Nichols, Rozae 64

O

Obama, Michelle 42, 108
ombré prints *64*, 188, *210*
Ono, Yoko *15*
Outerbridge, Paul *190*

P

Pac Man 164
Paris Haute Couture Week 200
Parsons The New School for Design 108, 166
Peter Pilotto 12, 158–63
    2011–12 (A/W) *159*
    2012 (A/W) *159*, *161*; (S/S) *162*
    2013 (S/S) *159*
Pheasant print *139*
Photoshop 12, 15, *134*, *146*, 200
Pilotto, Peter 12, 158–63
Plato's Atlantis 145, *145–6*, *149*
Plunkett, Anna *179*
Prabal Gurung 108–13
    2012 (A/W) *15*, *108*; (S/S) *108*
    2013 (Pre-Autumn) *112*; (Resort) 108, *111*
Prada 164–5
    2004–5 (A/W) *164*
    2008 (S/S) *164*
    2010 (S/S) 164, *164*
Prada, Mario 164
Prada, Miuccia 164
Prince, Richard *143*
Print Generator 159
Proenza Schouler 166–9
    2011 (S/S) *166*; (A/W) 166
    2012 (Pre-Autumn) 166
    2013 (S/S) 166, *166*, *168*
Pucci, Emilio 42, *210*
Pulitzer, Lilly 188

Q

Quake print *104*

R

RA Smart 10
recycled materials, fabrics made from *18*
Reva, Masha 170–7
Rhode Island School of Design 126
Richter, Gerhard *166*
Roberts, Alison 15, 34
Romance Was Born 178–87
    2011 (S/S) *179*
    2012 (S/S) *179*
    2013 (S/S) *179*, *186*

Royal Academy of Fine Arts, Antwerp 159, 205
Royal College of Art, London 91, 150

S

SABA 24
Sage, Russell 114
Saint Laurent, Yves 108
Sakkeus, Shane 103, *103*, *104*
Sales, Luke *179*
Saunders, Jonathan 12, 188–93
Scottish College of Textiles 114
Serra, Richard *136*
Shih Chien University 82
shirts *18*, *24*, *64*, *91*, *120*, *146*, *156*, *190*
shoes 53
shorts *69*, *186*
SHOWstudio.com 145
silk-screen printing 10, 34
Sistine Blue Rose print *108*
skirts 13, *38–9*, *58*, *63*, *82*, *85*, *91*, *98*, *100*, *104*, *131*,
    139, *150*, *166*, *190*, *202*
Smart, Alison 10
Smoke print *15*
socks *18*
sportswear *56*
St Martins School of Art 34
Steichen, Edward *130*
Stieglitz, Alfred *130*
Strip Valley prints *134*
Style.com 42
suits *18*, *100*, *108*
Swan Lake print *42*
Syndicate of Kiev *170*, *175*

T

Takada, Kenzo 58
Tatsuno, Koji 145
technical fabrics *33*, *108*, *117*, *120*
three-dimensional (3-D) printing 200, *202*
Thynn, Alexander *22*
Timbery, Esme *179*
Tisci, Riccardo 98
tops *58*, *96*, *98*, *139*, *150*
    peplum tops *33*
    shirts *18*, *24*, *64*, *91*, *120*, *146*, *156*, *190*
    sweatshirts *174*
    T-shirts *114*
    tunics *24*, *69*, *117*
    vests *104*
Topshop Unique 13, 194–99
    2011 (S/S) *4*, *10*, *15*

2012 (Christmas) *195*

2013 (S/S) 195; (A/W) *195*

trompe-l'oeil *131*

trouser suits *143*

trousers *4, 64, 69, 96*

Tsumori Chisato 58–63, 120

2011 (S/S) *60*

2012 (S/S) *58, 60, 63*; (A/W) *58*

Turlington Burns, Christy *24*

Tyler, Liv *100*

U

University of Lincoln 18

V

Van Beirendonck, Walter 205

Van Herpen, Iris 12, 200–3

Van Noten, Dries 120, 204–9

Van Saene, Dirk 205

Velosa, Joseph 210

Versace, Donatella 114

Versace, Gianni 91, 114

Versus 114

Victoria and Albert Museum 150, *205*

Vim print *34*

Vreeland, Diana 150

W

Warhol, Andy *70*

Watanabe, Junya 58

Water print *103*

Weber, Bruce 114

Westwood, Vivienne 15

White, Clarence *130*

Widrig, Daniel 200

Williamson, Matthew 210–13, 214

Y

Yamamoto, Yohji 58, 126

Yee, Marina 205

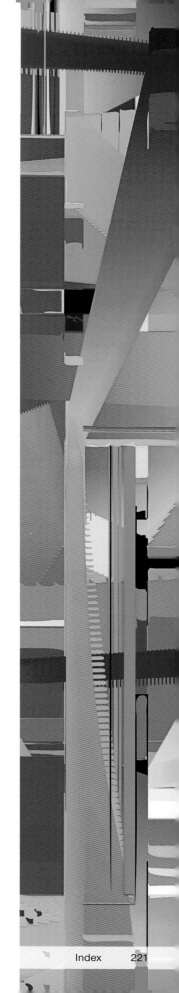

Author's Acknowledgements

I would especially like to thank Fleet Bigwood for sharing his wisdom and time. Thanks also to the following for their informed and inspiring insights:

Philip Delamore
Eline Le Callennec
Pascale Gueracague
Caroline Kelly
Emma Mawston
Meera Sleight
Alison Smart

Finally, thank you to James and Pearl Hawke for their patience and newly-found appreciation for printed texiles.

Bibliography

Digital Textile Design (second edition), Melanie Bowles and Ceri Isaac, Laurence King Publishing, 2012.

Digital Visions for Fashion and Textiles, Sarah E Braddock Clarke and Jane Harris, Thames & Hudson, 2012.

Fashion Futures, Bradley Quinn, Merrell, 2012.

Fashionable Technology: The Intersection of Design, Fashion, Science and Technology, Sabine Seymour, Springer, 2009.

Techno Textiles 2: Revolutionary Fabrics for Fashion and Design, Sarah E Braddock Clarke and Marie O'Mahoney, Thames & Hudson, 2007.

www.SHOWstudio.com

www.fashiondigitalstudio.com

www.sty!e.com

www.patternbank.com

Picture Credits

The publishers would like to thank the following sources for their kind permission to reproduce the pictures in this book.

Key: t=Top, b=Bottom, c=Centre, l=Left and r=Right

Agi & Sam: 18, 20, 21tl, 21tc, 21bl, 21cb, 21br, 22, 23, 216, 217, 222, 223

Image Courtesy Michael Angel ©: 29, 31r, /Illustration by Michael Angel ©: 30, 31l, /Campaign Photo by Christopher Katke ©: 25, 32-33, 33, /Photo by Christopher Katke ©: 26l, 26r, 27l, 27r

Antoni & Alison: 34-35, 35br, 36-37, 38, 39, 40t, 40b, 41t, 41b

Basso & Brooke: 12, 42-43, 43 (inset), 44, 45, 46-47, 48, 48-49, 50, 51, 218, 219, 220, 221

Camera Press: 11, 19, 21tr, 59, 60, 61l, 61r, 70, 72r, 76, 77, 78-79, 92l, 92r, 93, 96, 97, 98, 99, 100, 108, 115, 116l, 116r, 120, 130, 132tl, 135 (inset), 137, 138l, 138r, 139, 142, 148, 149, 150, 151, 155bl, 155bc, 155br, 158, 162, 163l, 163r, 164-165, 167, 168, 169, 190, 191, 203, 204, 207r, 208, 211, 212r, 213l, /Jamie Baker: 7, /Matteo Bazzi: 81, /ED/CE/Locog: 74-75, /Tristan Gregory: 114, /Mitchell Sams: 80, 101l, 101r, 146r, 192-193, 203, 209, /Anthea Simms: 52, 54l, 54r, 55l, 55r, 72l, 73l, 73r, 117, 124, 125, 130-131, 131r, 133br, 144, 144-145, 146l, 152, 153, 155tl, 155tc, 155tr, 188, 212l, 213r, /R.Stonehouse: 189

Hussein Chalayan: 53, 56, 94-95

Clover Canyon: 2, 16-17, 64, 65l, 65r, 66-67, 68l, 68r, 69

Corbis: /Britta Pedersen/epa: 202, /© Fairchild Photo Service/Condé Nast: 118, 119l, 119r, 121, 122, 123, 166, 201

Fabitoria: 82, 83t, 83b, 84, 85, 86-87, 88-89

Holly Fulton: 90, 91

Getty Images: 28, 105l, 184t, 186, 187, /AFP: 132tr, 132br, 178-179, /IMG: 24, /Gamma-Rapho: 126, 132bl, WireImage: 133tl, 133tr, 133bl

Josh Goot: 102-103, 104, 105r, 106-107

Pascale Gueracague: 140-141

Prabal Gurung: 110-111, 112-113

Eline Le Callennec: 13, 135 (bkgd)

Shane McAdams: 214t (bkgd), 214b (bkgd), 215 (bkgd)

MOD Photographic: /© Morgan O'Donovan: 57, 128, 128-129, 134, 156, 157, 159, 160-161, 210

Mark Reay: 15

Masha Reva: 170, 171, 172, 173, 174-175, 176-177, 224

Romance Was Born: 180-181, 184bl, 184cb, 184br, 185

Sonny Photos: 58, 62-63, 63, 102, 109, 147, 182-183, 205, 206-207

Topshop: 4-5, 14, 194, 195, 196-197, 198-199

www.helpmystyle.ie: 127

Matthew Williamson: 214t (inset), 214b (inset), 215 (insets)

Every effort has been made to acknowledge correctly and contact the source and/or copyright holder of each picture and Carlton Books Limited apologizes for any unintentional errors or omissions, which will be corrected in future editions of this book.